New COMFORT COOKING

HOMESTYLE KETO RECIPES THAT WON'T BUST YOUR BELT OR WALLET

MICHAEL SILVERSTEIN

Celebrity Chef and Author of *New Keto Cooking*

PAGE STREET
PUBLISHING CO.

PAGE STREET
PUBLISHING CO.

First published in 2021 by
Page Street Publishing Co.
27 Congress Street, Suite 105
Salem, MA 01970
www.pagestreetpublishing.com

Distributed by Macmillan, sales in Canada by The Canadian Manda Group.

25 24 23 22 21   1 2 3 4 5

ISBN-13: 978-1-64567-456-6
ISBN-10: 1-64567-456-8

Library of Congress Control Number: 2021931966

Cover and book design by Page Street Publishing Co.
Photography by Michael Silverstein
Cover Photography by Dan Galvan
"Chef Michael" Logo by Artsy Tessy
Sanyu Kyeyune, Contributing Editor

Printed and bound in the United States of America

FOR MY PARENTS

To Mom, who first inspired my passion for cooking and
taught me to never stop fighting for what I believe in.
To Dad, who showed me how to follow my dreams and the
importance of a good laugh. I love you both so much.

contents

Introduction   6

Cook Like a Pro   8

WINNER, WINNER, CHICKEN DINNERS   15

Pickle-Brined Crispy Chicken Tendies with Homemade Ranch   16

Sweet & Sour Baked BBQ Chicken   19

Sticky "Hot Honey" Chicken Wings   20

Chinese Restaurant Sesame Chicken   23

Rich & Creamy Indian Butter Chicken   24

Classic Italian Chicken Marsala   27

Filipino-Inspired Chicken Adobo   28

Homestyle Chicken-Bacon-Ranch Skillet   31

Sheet Pan Pesto Chicken with Jammy Tomatoes   32

Smoky Southwest Chicken Picante   35

YOU GOTTA BEEF WITH ME?   37

Famous French Onion Meatloaf—Upgraded!   38

Jalapeño Popper–Stuffed Burgers with "Animal Sauce"   41

Crispy Garlic Butter Steak   42

Giant Showstopping Meatballs in Rosé Sauce   45

Grilled Carne Asada with Homemade Salsa Roja   46

Philly Cheesesteak—Hold the Bun!   49

Low & Slow Texas Brisket Chili   50

A Little Fancy Steak au Poivre   53

Brisket for the Holidays   54

BRINGING HOME THE BACON   57

The Best Damn Keto Pizza Ever!   58

Fall-Off-the-Bone Ribs with Mike's Coffee Dry Rub   61

Million-Dollar Lasagna Roll-Ups   62

Slow Cooker BBQ Pulled Pork   65

Sausage, Peppers, & Onions with Spicy Creole Aioli   66

Guilt-Free Creamy Pasta Florentine   69

KEEPIN' IT REEL   71

Garlic Lovers' Shrimp Scampi   72

Crispy Fried Fish Tacos with Baja Sauce   75

Stunning Brown Butter Shrimp & Grits   76

Sweet Teriyaki-Glazed Salmon   79

Sugarless Shrimp Pad Thai   80

Blackened Salmon in Creamy Cajun Sauce   83

Pepper-Crusted Tuna Steak with Sesame Ginger Chimichurri   84

SOUP FOR THE SOUL   87

Cozy Loaded "Potato" Soup   88

Quick & Easy Clam Chowder   91

Bread Shop Broccoli Cheddar Soup   92

5-Hour Short Rib Beef Stew   95

Mom's Chicken Soup   96

"Hangover" Beef Pho   99

Curried Butternut Squash Bisque   100

EAT YOUR VEGGIES!   103

Cheesy Low-Carb Scalloped "Potatoes"   104

Crack Brussels Sprouts with Honey Mustard Sauce   107

No Big Dill "Potato" Salad   108

Belly-Warming Baked Broccoli Alfredo   111

Garlic Parmesan Green Beans   112

Creamy Smoked Cheddar "Grits"   115

Cauliflower Dirty Rice   116

Bacon & Bleu Coleslaw   119

A LITTLE SOMETHIN' SWEET   121

Ooey Gooey Double Chocolate Brownies   122

Cinnamon Roll Cheesecake Bites   125

Lemon Pound Cake with Lemony Cream Cheese Glaze   126

Velvety Peanut Butter Cup Mousse with Homemade Chocolate Sauce   129

No-Churn Mint Chocolate Chip Ice Cream   130

Triple Berry Crisp   133

Coconut Cake with Coconut Cream Cheese Frosting   134

Magical Strawberry Icebox Pie   137

THE (NOT-SO-BASIC) BASICS   139

Low-Carb Cheddar Bay Biscuits   140

Cheesy Garlic Breadsticks   143

Keto Cornbread   144

Fluffy Waffles & Pancakes   147

Crispy Rosemary Sea Salt Crackers   148

WHEN I DIP, YOU DIP, WE DIP   151

Buffalo Chicken Pimento Dip   152

Restaurant-Style White Queso   155

Everything-but-the-Bagel Dip   156

Spicy Maryland Crab Dip   159

Greek Roasted Garlic & Feta Dip   160

About the Author   163

Acknowledgments   164

Index   165

INTRODUCTION

The symphony of the pots and pans clanging and the distinct smell of the onions cooking are still vivid to me, as I remember the hours my mom spent perfecting her chicken soup (page 96). I can still feel the wobbling step stool and the cold countertop, barely at my chin, as I joyfully stirred the brownie batter, waiting for my turn to lick the spoon. I can perfectly remember feeling squished between the folding chairs at the "kids table" with my cousins, as my dad carved the brisket (page 54) during the holidays.

Despite both of my parents' busy work schedules, family dinner every night was not up for debate. I think back to that one time of the day we would all spend together, talking, eating, and, for my sisters and me, skillfully dodging the age-old question, "How was school today?" These moments taught me that sharing a meal is how you say "I love you" to the important people in your life.

Today, nothing brings me more joy than seeing someone smile after their first bite of my food. So, this book is my way of sitting down to dinner with you, sharing a good meal, a story, and, perhaps, a smile. This is also a collection of recipes to help ensure you love every bite of the food you're eating, without sacrificing your health.

I've spent years cooking, perfecting my culinary skills—not to mention learning a few things from Gordon Ramsay while competing on MasterChef—and, after going Keto, I knew I could put those skills to work, re-creating the dishes we all love but with careful consideration of how those foods could affect us. Most of the traditional comfort foods we know are generally very unhealthy, so I had to change that. I fell in love with the Ketogenic diet specifically because it allows me to make satisfying meals, using whole ingredients like meat, fish, and veggies. I could create hearty, filling dishes, rather than restricting myself to the traditional "diet foods." In fact, I lost over 80 pounds (36 kg) in one year just from food like this, and I have kept it off since. And helping others do the same is a definite passion of mine.

For so many of us, childhood favorites inevitably become our comfort foods as adults. But we can also form new and surprising food memories every day. Have you ever taken a bite of something new and thought, "Wow, I've never had anything like this before!"? Well, this book is designed to create more of those "aha" moments for you. I want to celebrate food and all of its unique flavors, spices, and origins. Every recipe is designed to bring you the feeling of "home," wherever and whoever you are, and that's what comfort food is really supposed to do.

Whether it's chicken tenders (page 16) or pho (page 99), each dish is like a warm hug. I hope you find nostalgia in this book. But I also hope you discover something new that creates exciting food memories that will stay with you and your family for life.

Packed with low-carb, sugar-free, and gluten-free recipes—many of which are also nut-free and dairy-free—this book is full of feel-good food for anyone, Keto or not. Delicious, healthy, real meals that will fill you up, nourish you, and bring some comfort to your dinner table. This is not a diet book. This is not a weight-loss book. These are easy-to-make dishes your entire family will love and feel better about eating. This is food that will give you a smile, without busting your belt. So, what are you waiting for? Roll up those sleeves, and let's get cooking!

COOK LIKE A PRO

Here are some tips, tricks, and resources to keep you cooking like a chef in your kitchen. And keep your eyes open for more Pro Tips peppered—pun intended—throughout the recipes in the book. I want you to cook with ease and confidence, and these tips will help you do that!

MISE EN PLACE

Read the recipe all the way through before you start cooking, and prep all your veggies in advance. It also helps to pre-measure and pre-chop all your ingredients, and get out all the equipment you'll need for the recipe as well. This is called mise en place and lets you focus on the timing and execution while you're cooking.

PRACTICE, PRACTICE, PRACTICE

If you're a bit nervous in the kitchen, that's OK! Getting comfortable in the kitchen takes time, and I'll certainly help you get more confident with each recipe in this book.

But first, let's sharpen those skills! I recommend buying a bag of onions or peppers for a couple of dollars and practicing your way through the entire bag: Of course, save or freeze all those cut veggies for later! Check out the knife cuts on the next page and practice them until you feel comfortable. You don't need to move quickly, but just getting used to holding the knife and feeling comfortable is key.

In terms of knives, you don't need a big, fancy set that costs hundreds of dollars. All you really need to make fantastic food is one decent chef's knife. Just make sure you are using a thick plastic or wooden cutting board—not glass—and never run your knife through the dishwasher or leave it in your sink to get rusty and banged up. After you use it, simply wash it right away with water and soap, and leave it out to air dry. Store your knife in a safe place, like a knife block, and it will last you a lifetime.

Ironically, a sharp knife is the best way to prevent yourself from getting cut, as a dull knife can easily slip off the food you're slicing. So, keep your knife sharp—I send my knives out once a year to get professionally sharpened. It usually costs about $10 per knife. You can enter "knife sharpening" into your favorite internet search engine and find companies that will even send an envelope right to your door. So, you can ship your knives out for sharpening without ever leaving your home.

ROUGH CHOP   CHOP   DICE   MINCE

SLICE   THIN SLICE   JULIENNE   CHIFFONADE

KNIFE CUTS

You'll notice some terminology in the ingredient lists throughout this book, so above is a quick culinary guide to the most common knife cuts you'll need to know. Go to my YouTube channel for a quick lesson on knife skills: www.youtube.com/chefmichael.

KEEPING TIDY

The most unexciting Pro Tip ever, I know, but it's just true. Clean your kitchen as you go. While you are cooking, there are always brief moments of free time, while water boils or while something sears or bakes, for instance. Take advantage of each of these moments, and wipe the countertop or put away some used ingredients. A clean workspace will help you focus on your food, and it will make you a better home cook. I promise.

SWEETENER GUIDE

Sugar substitutes are a controversial topic for people on a Keto or sugar-free diet. It's a very personal decision, and you'll have to do a little self-experimentation to find out which sweetener is right for you and your body. You may find that a given sweetener gives you a stomachache or leaves a bad aftertaste, but that will vastly differ from person to person. Here are the four sweeteners I'd recommend you use; they have a low glycemic impact—the effect on blood glucose and insulin levels—and are generally considered safe to use. That said, if a recipe in this book suggests a specific sweetener, use that one, as the recipe may not work using another sweetener. If it says "granulated sweetener," for instance, you can use the sweetener of your choice.

ALLULOSE—Allulose is a new low-calorie sugar substitute on the market. It's called a rare sugar, because it's found only in small quantities in nature, in fruits like figs and raisins. It's my personal go-to, because it cooks and caramelizes the most like real sugar. It has a great taste, but is still generally harder to find than the others, though it's starting to pop up in more and more regular supermarkets. I order mine on Amazon for the best pricing. Note: It's not yet available in Canada or Europe.

ERYTHRITOL—A sugar alcohol, found in products like Swerve, erythritol is a good sugar-free option and works well in baking, but it leaves many people with a "cooling" aftertaste, and tends to crystallize in sauces and liquids. Note: It will not properly caramelize, so be careful with this one in caramel sauces or desserts.

MONK FRUIT—Another good option, but monk fruit is often blended with other sweeteners, so read the product labels. It can have a strong aftertaste to many people as well, but it's a great natural option.

STEVIA—Naturally derived from the stevia leaf, stevia sweeteners, especially liquid stevia, can be around 100 times sweeter than sugar, so use it sparingly. Note: For some, stevia has a strong aftertaste, but try it for yourself.

SWEETENERS TO AVOID—Maltitol, maltodextrin, sucralose, aspartame, dextrose, and fructose. Many of these can be very harsh on your gut and can spike your blood sugar much like sugar does.

SALT GUIDE

SEA SALT OR PINK SALT—Made from evaporated seawater, it is by far the most nutritious salt, due to its diverse mineral and electrolyte content. It has a complex flavor as well. I prefer Redmond sea salt, which is made in the US, as it is free of microplastics, unlike many of the Himalayan salts mined abroad. But any sea salt or pink Himalayan salt is generally a great choice.

KOSHER SALT—Due to its large crystal size, it is not as salty as table or sea salt by volume. If a recipe calls for sea salt, you can use kosher salt, but use about one-third extra to compensate for the lower salinity. It's also very inexpensive and is the preferred salt of restaurant chefs for its ease of use. It's also particularly good for seasoning a steak or fish, as the large crystals stick really nicely to raw meat.

FLAKY (FINISHING) SALT—This is used on top of a finished dish, like steak. It's very expensive and has a large, pyramid-like structure. It adds not only flavor but texture to a dish, only to be used at the end. There are flavor-infused finishing salts, as well. I love Maldon Smoked Sea Salt for its wonderful smoky aroma.

TABLE SALT (IODIZED)—This salt is very high in sodium—it's basically pure NaCl—low in nutritional value, and, frankly, tastes terrible. Have you ever tasted it by itself? Yuck! Avoid using it in your cooking if you can.

FAT IS YOUR FRIEND

The various oils and fats each have unique smoke points—the temperature at which they start to burn. Using the right oil is important both for your cooking and for your health. Use the guide below for your cooking.

	SMOKE POINT	SUGGESTED USE	FLAVOR
BUTTER	302°F (150°C)	Low heat, pan sauces, baking	Creamy, savory
GHEE	482°F (250°C)	Frying, searing, curries	Cheesy, bold
VEGETABLE, CANOLA, PEANUT, GRAPESEED OILS	400–453°F (204–234°C)	Avoid using these, due to inflammatory properties	Neutral
AVOCADO OIL	520°F (271°C)	High-heat frying and deep-frying	Mild, nutty
OLIVE OIL	320°F (160°C)	Roasting, using cold, and in dressings	Fruity, spicy, flavorful
ANIMAL FAT (BACON, LARD, TALLOW)	370–400°F (188–204°C)	Roasting, panfrying, deep-frying	Flavorful, complex
COCONUT OIL	350°F (177°C)	Sautéing, roasting, curries	Coconut flavor
SESAME OIL	350°F (177°C)	Finishing, best used raw and in dressings	Intense, nutty

TEMP YOUR MEATS

The secret to restaurant-quality meat is cooking it to the right temperature. Below are the recommended minimum internal temperatures for the various types of meat. The easiest way to guarantee perfectly cooked meat every time is to use a meat thermometer or instant-read thermometer. You can buy them online for around $10, if you don't have one. And, remember to always let your meat rest, so that it retains its juiciness when you cut into it.

BEEF*	Steak (Flank, Strip, Ribeye, Porterhouse, T-bone)	130°F (54°C)
	Filet Mignon	125°F (52°C)
	Prime Rib	120°F (49°C)
	Meatloaf	160°F (71°C)
	Burgers	135°F (57°C)
PORK*	Pork Chops	140°F (60°C)
	Tenderloin	135°F (57°C)
CHICKEN	All Chicken	165°F (74°C)
FISH	Salmon	120°F (49°C)
	All Other Fish	140°F (60°C)
GAME MEATS*	Lamb and Goat	125°F (52°C)
	Duck Breast	130°F (54°C)
	Veal	135°F (57°C)
	Rabbit	145°F (63°C)
	Venison	135°F (57°C)

*Note: These temperatures are for medium-rare. For more medium temperatures, add 5°F (15°C). The temperatures above produce the tastiest results, though some of them are below what the USDA recommends. According to the USDA, consuming raw or undercooked meats, poultry, seafood, shellfish, or eggs may increase your risk of foodborne illness, especially if you have certain medical conditions.

MACROS

You'll notice that I've included the macros, or macronutrients, for each recipe in this book. For many people, calculating and tracking macros for their food is an important part of maintaining a healthy lifestyle. However, it's important to note that the precise nutritional breakdown for any recipe depends on the exact brands you use of a particular ingredient or the precise size of a given vegetable, for example.

Make sure to read those labels when buying groceries! Often, companies have hidden ingredients in their products, like sugars or flours. So, turn that package around and read those ingredients.

For those practicing a Ketogenic lifestyle, the carbohydrates in a given recipe are particularly important for maintaining a metabolic state of ketosis, which occurs when your body switches to ketones as fuel, rather than sugars. These recipes include both the "net carbs" and the "total carbs," which can be very confusing for those new to this lifestyle. So below is a simple equation for calculating the net carbs in any recipe or food product.

Net Carbs = Total Carbs – Fiber – Sugar Alcohols/Allulose

WINNER, WINNER, chicken DINNERS

The days of boring chicken dishes are over! Eating healthier does not mean a sad, dry piece of chicken on a salad. In this chapter, I'll show you how to have all your favorite chicken dishes and still fit them into your Keto lifestyle without losing any of the yumminess. So, whether it's Chinese Restaurant Sesame Chicken (page 23) or Pickle-Brined Crispy Chicken Tendies with Homemade Ranch (page 16), these easy dishes are so egg-cellent, your whole family will be gobbling up seconds.

Pickle-Brined Crispy Chicken Tendies with Homemade Ranch	16
Sweet & Sour Baked BBQ Chicken	19
Sticky "Hot Honey" Chicken Wings	20
Chinese Restaurant Sesame Chicken	23
Rich & Creamy Indian Butter Chicken	24
Classic Italian Chicken Marsala	27
Filipino-Inspired Chicken Adobo	28
Homestyle Chicken-Bacon-Ranch Skillet	31
Sheet Pan Pesto Chicken with Jammy Tomatoes	32
Smoky Southwest Chicken Picante	35

CHICKEN TENDERS

2 lbs (910 g) chicken tenders

1½ cups (360 ml) pickle juice

½ cup (120 ml) buttermilk (optional)

½ cup (120 g) mayonnaise

1½ cups (110 g) unseasoned pork crumbs (see Pro Tip)

½ cup (15 g) grated Parmesan cheese

2 tsp (6 g) garlic powder

Oil, for deep-frying (optional)

EASY RANCH DRESSING

¼ cup (60 g) mayonnaise

¼ cup (60 g) sour cream

2 tsp (10 ml) water or buttermilk

½ tsp dried dill

½ tsp dried parsley

1 tsp garlic powder

1 tsp black pepper

MACROS PER SERVING

Calories: 707 | Protein: 67 g

Fat: 45.3 g | Net Carbs: 2.4 g

Fiber: 1.1 g | Sugar Alcohol: 0 g

Total Carbs: 3.5 g

Pro Tip:
Can't find pork crumbs? You can easily make your own. Simply blitz plain pork rinds—chicharrón—in a food processor to make pork panko quickly and very cheaply.

Serves 4 people

Pickle-Brined Crispy Chicken Tendies with Homemade Ranch

For the record, chicken tenders are not just for kids. And these grown-up tenders have a secret ingredient: pickle juice. Don't throw away the leftover pickle juice in that jar! Not only does it give the chicken an amazing flavor, but it makes it unbelievably tender and juicy as well. And the air fryer makes this recipe extra easy—and healthy! No air fryer? No problem. I've also included instructions for deep-frying the tenders.

Add the chicken, pickle juice, and buttermilk (if using) to a large bowl, and wrap it tightly with plastic wrap. Marinate the chicken in the fridge for at least 2 hours, but no more than 24 hours.

Make the ranch dressing while the chicken marinates. In a small mixing bowl, combine the mayo, sour cream, water or buttermilk, dill, parsley, garlic powder, and pepper. Cover the bowl with plastic wrap and refrigerate the dressing until you're ready to use it.

To cook the chicken, drain off the brine and pat the chicken tenders completely dry with paper towels. Place the chicken tenders in a gallon-sized (3.8-L) resealable plastic bag. Add the mayo, seal the bag, and use your hands to massage the mayo all over the chicken, so they're completely coated.

Preheat your air fryer to 400°F (204°C). In a wide bowl, add the pork crumbs, Parmesan, and garlic, and mix the ingredients well with a fork. Then dip each piece of chicken from the bag into the crumb mixture, pressing the chicken into the crumbs to create a nice, even coating.

Once all the chicken is coated, add it to the tray of the air fryer in one layer—do not overcrowd the air fryer or the chicken will steam instead of crisp. You may need to cook the chicken in two batches. Air fry the chicken for 15 minutes, flipping halfway through, or until it's golden brown and crispy. Once it's finished, let the chicken cool down on a cooling rack before serving it.

Optionally, you can deep-fry the chicken tenders instead. Simply warm up a small pot with about 1 cup (240 ml) of oil until a thermometer reads 350°F (180°C), then fry the chicken for about 5 minutes, or until it's crispy.

3 lbs (1.4 kg) bone-in chicken quarters (4 pieces)

1 cup (240 ml) sugar-free BBQ sauce (I prefer Ray's No Sugar Added brand; see Pro Tip)

1½ cups (360 ml) Italian dressing

1 large turnip or 2 carrots, cut into ¾-inch (2-cm) pieces

1 yellow onion, cut into ½-inch (1.3-cm) slices and rings separated

4 whole cloves garlic

3 bay leaves

¼ tsp black pepper

MACROS PER SERVING

Calories: 520 | Protein: 68.2 g
Fat: 19.6 g | Net Carbs: 10.1 g
Fiber: 3.5 g | Sugar Alcohol: 0 g
Total Carbs: 13.6 g

Serves 4 people

Sweet & Sour Baked BBQ Chicken

This baked BBQ chicken recipe is a replica of a dish my mom made us growing up. The unexpected combination of BBQ sauce and Italian salad dressing creates a perfect harmony of sweet, smoky, and tangy—you're just going to have to trust me on this one. And this one-pan dinner is packed with veggies, so no need to make a side dish here. The turnips make the perfect low-carb substitute for the potatoes my mom would use in the original recipe.

Start by removing your chicken from the fridge 30 minutes ahead of cooking. Then, preheat your oven to 375°F (190°C).

In a large 9 x 13–inch (23 x 33–cm) baking dish, stir to combine the BBQ sauce and the Italian dressing. Add in the chicken, tossing it in the sauce to coat it, then leaving it skin side up. Add in the turnip or carrots, onion, and cloves of garlic, stirring again to coat everything in the sauce. Spread the veggies evenly around the spaces between the chicken. Slide in the bay leaves around the dish, and top the dish evenly with the pepper.

Cover the dish tightly with aluminum foil, and bake it for 30 minutes. Remove the foil and bake the dish for 30 minutes uncovered, or until the internal temperature of the chicken is 165°F (74°C) on an instant-read thermometer inserted into the thickest part; baste the chicken with the sauce every 10 minutes. Remove the dish from the oven, and let the chicken rest for at least 10 minutes. Remove the bay leaves before serving.

Pro Tip: Instead of using store-bought sugar-free BBQ sauce, try making your own! Check out the homemade sugar-free hickory BBQ sauce on page 65.

BAKED WINGS

1 tsp sea salt

½ tsp black pepper

1 tsp paprika

1 tsp onion powder

1 tbsp (9 g) garlic powder

1 tbsp (15 g) baking powder

2 lbs (910 g) chicken wings, flats and drumettes

"HOT HONEY" SAUCE

¼ cup (60 ml) Valentina's Hot Sauce, or your favorite hot sauce

½ tsp yellow mustard

1 tbsp (15 g) sugar-free ketchup

1 tbsp (15 ml) apple cider vinegar

2 tbsp (30 g) unsalted butter

½ cup (96 g) allulose sweetener

1 tbsp (15 ml) soy sauce or coconut aminos

FOR SERVING

Celery sticks and ranch or bleu cheese dressing (optional)

MACROS PER SERVING

Calories: 467 | Protein: 51.9 g

Fat: 20.9 g | Net Carbs: 2.9 g

Fiber: 0.7 g | Sugar Alcohol: 24 g

Total Carbs: 27.6 g

Serves 3 people

Sticky "Hot Honey" Chicken Wings

I love some good wings! Sadly, many of the wings we order from restaurants are coated in flour or cornstarch and sugary sauce, so this recipe is a great way to make hot wings fit a low-carb and sugar-free lifestyle. Crispy, juicy, sweet, and spicy, this recipe is punch-you-in-the-face good. Perfect for dinner any night of the week, but especially great for game day, these wings are seriously good eats.

Try pairing this with the No Big Dill "Potato" Salad (page 108).

Preheat your oven to 300°F (149°C). Prepare a baking sheet with a baking rack, and set it aside.

In a large mixing bowl, add the sea salt, pepper, paprika, onion powder, garlic powder, and baking powder. Mix well to combine. Pat the chicken wings dry with paper towels, and add them to the mixing bowl with the spices. Toss the chicken wings in the bowl, making sure all of the spices are evenly distributed all over the chicken. Then place the wings on the baking rack in one even layer. Bake the wings for 30 minutes, flipping them halfway through.

Make the sauce while the chicken is baking. Combine the hot sauce, mustard, ketchup, vinegar, butter, allulose, and soy sauce or coconut aminos in a small saucepan. Bring the sauce to a boil over medium heat, stirring. Let the sauce simmer for 5 minutes, or until it's slightly thick. Set it aside.

Once the chicken has cooked for 30 minutes, turn up the heat to broil, and let the chicken wings cook for 3 to 5 minutes. Take the pan out of the oven, flip each chicken wing over, and return the pan to the oven for 3 to 5 minutes, or until the wings are golden brown and crispy. Then, use a large mixing bowl to toss the wings in the hot sauce.

Serve the wings with the celery sticks and ranch or bleu cheese dressing, if using—I am firmly Team Bleu Cheese.

Pro Tip: For extra crispy wings, make the wings in an air fryer instead. Simply cook them at 400°F (204°C) for 20 to 25 minutes, rotating them halfway through.

CRISPY CHICKEN

2 lbs (910 g) boneless, skinless chicken thighs, cut into 1-inch (3-cm) cubes

2 tbsp (30 g) baking powder

2 tbsp (10 g) coconut flour

2 tbsp (30 ml) soy sauce or coconut aminos

1 tsp garlic powder

2 egg whites

2 cups (480 ml) avocado or frying oil (see Pro Tip)

SESAME SAUCE

5 cloves garlic, chopped

1 tbsp (13 g) peeled, chopped fresh ginger

⅓ cup (80 ml) soy sauce or coconut aminos

1 cup (192 g) allulose sweetener

3 tbsp (45 g) sugar-free ketchup

2 tbsp (20 g) sesame seeds

3 tbsp (45 ml) sesame oil

FOR SERVING

Thinly sliced scallions (optional)

MACROS PER SERVING

Calories: 618 | Protein: 50.2 g
Fat: 40.4 g | Net Carbs: 8.7 g
Fiber: 1.3 g | Sugar Alcohol: 48 g
Total Carbs: 58 g

Serves 4 people

Chinese Restaurant Sesame Chicken

My favorite meal growing up came from the local Chinese restaurant near our home. We nicknamed it "George's" after the owner, who lived down the street from us. And it remains today the best Chinese food in the country—don't try to convince me otherwise. This sugar-free and low-carb version of sesame chicken is perfectly sweet and tangy, and brings me right back home to Maryland. I like serving this with a side of steamed cauliflower rice.

Combine the chicken thighs, baking powder, coconut flour, soy sauce, garlic powder, and egg whites in a mixing bowl; mix well. Let the mixture marinate in the fridge for 20 minutes.

Make the sauce while the chicken marinates. Combine the garlic, ginger, soy sauce, allulose, and ketchup in a small bowl.

Line a plate with paper towels and set it aside. In a large pot or wok over high heat, bring the oil up to 350°F (180°C), using a thermometer to check the temperature. Add in half the chicken mixture, stir to remove any clumps of chicken, and fry for 5 minutes, or until the chicken is golden brown. Remove the first batch, and place it on a plate to rest. Meanwhile, fry the second half of the chicken, and repeat. Carefully remove the oil from the pan (see Pro Tip).

Place the same pot over high heat. Once the pot is hot, pour in the sauce mixture, and cook it for 3 minutes, or until the sauce is rapidly bubbling. Turn off the heat and add the sesame seeds and chicken, stirring well to evenly coat the chicken. Then stir in the sesame oil. The chicken will be nice and glossy.

Serve the chicken in bowls, topped with the scallions, if using.

Pro Tip: Especially if you're using a quality oil like avocado oil, it gets expensive, so don't waste it. Save the frying oil for later, as you can use it to fry again. Simply pour the used oil into a large jar or bottle through a mesh sieve. It will last in your pantry, out of direct sunlight, for several months.

BUTTER CHICKEN

¼ cup (60 g) ghee or unsalted butter

1 yellow onion, chopped

4 cloves garlic, minced

1 tbsp (6 g) garam masala

⅛–½ tsp cayenne, to taste

3 tbsp (48 g) tomato paste

1 (8-oz [227-g]) can tomato sauce

½ cup (120 ml) heavy whipping cream

2 tbsp (30 g) unsalted butter

2 tbsp (24 g) granulated sweetener

½ tsp sea salt

1 lb (455 g) boneless chicken breast, cut into ¾-inch (2-cm) cubes

FOR SERVING

Plain Indian or Greek yogurt, cilantro leaves, and/or steamed cauliflower rice (optional)

MACROS PER SERVING

Calories: 493 | Protein: 52.5 g

Fat: 28.1 g | Net Carbs: 6.6 g

Fiber: 1.9 g | Sugar Alcohol: 8 g

Total Carbs: 16.5 g

Rich & Creamy Indian Butter Chicken

Indian food may just be my favorite cuisine in the world. After traveling through India, I was blown away by the richness and depth of the food and the sheer vastness of the cuisine across each region of the country. So, I wanted to bring you a recipe that's easy and quick enough for you to make at home but brings you all the beauty of an Indian-style dish. Butter chicken, or murgh makhani, was developed in Delhi in the 1950s and typically takes hours to make by marinating the chicken and making a special spice blend. This version certainly cuts corners from the original, but it has all the same cozy flavors, and it's wonderfully creamy, buttery, and slightly sweet. Oh, and did I mention it uses butter twice? Feel free to swap out the chicken breast for chicken thighs, cubed lamb, or even paneer. And serve it with your favorite rice substitute on the side to keep it low-carb. You can also make this dairy-free by swapping the heavy whipping cream and butter for coconut cream and oil.

Melt the ghee in a large saucepan with a lid over medium-high heat. Once it's hot, add the onion. Sauté the onion for 3 minutes, then add the garlic, garam masala, and cayenne. Stir the spices and garlic continuously to toast them for about 60 seconds, or until fragrant; you don't want them to burn. Add the tomato paste and continue stirring for 30 seconds, then add the tomato sauce, cream, butter, sweetener, and salt. Stir well, and bring the mixture up to a gentle simmer.

Turn the heat down to medium-low, and add in the chicken. Let the pot simmer for 15 minutes, or until the chicken is firm and opaque white, stirring occasionally to prevent the sauce from burning on the bottom.

To serve, drizzle the top of the chicken with the yogurt, sprinkle with cilantro, and serve with a side of cauliflower rice, if using.

SEARED CHICKEN

1½ lbs (680 g) thin-sliced chicken breasts (see Pro Tip)

½ tbsp (9 g) sea salt

½ tsp black pepper

2 tbsp (30 ml) avocado oil

MARSALA SAUCE

6 tbsp (90 g) unsalted butter, divided

4 cloves garlic, minced

1 small shallot, minced

½ cup (120 ml) dry Marsala wine or sherry

½ cup (120 ml) chicken broth

½ tsp sea salt

¼ tsp xanthan gum

1 lb (455 g) cremini mushrooms, sliced

FOR SERVING

Chopped fresh parsley and shaved Parmesan cheese (optional)

MACROS PER SERVING

Calories: 476 | Protein: 39.9 g
Fat: 28.4 g | Net Carbs: 6.8 g
Fiber: 2.4 g | Sugar Alcohol: 0 g
Total Carbs: 9.2 g

Pro Tip: If you can't find thin-sliced chicken, you can always pound out boneless chicken breasts or tenders using a 1-gallon (3.8-L) resealable plastic bag and a rolling pin.

Serves 4 people

Classic Italian Chicken Marsala

My first job was at a local Italian restaurant in my town. I was 13 years old and too young to actually work, so I polished silverware and rolled napkins for hours, and I loved it; the owner would even slip me a cash tip at the end of the shift. The chorus of the chefs barking orders, the sight of plate after plate flying through the "pass": This was my first exposure to the restaurant industry, and I was immediately hooked. I started paying close attention to the chefs, which turned into my first culinary lessons. I first learned how to make chicken marsala—and so much more—at that restaurant. I can still picture the chefs pouring the wine from the large green bottles onto the pans as they would light up in flames. This Ketofied classic recipe is a take on what I learned at a young age. Packed with mushrooms and a rich sauce, this recipe is quick and easy, and definitely feeds a crowd. I like to serve this family-style, with some bread to soak up all that sauce.

Try pairing this with the Cheesy Garlic Breadsticks (page 143).

For the chicken, evenly coat both sides of the chicken with the salt and pepper. In a 12-inch (31-cm) skillet, warm the avocado oil over high heat. Once it's hot, fry the chicken for 60 to 90 seconds on each side, or just until it's golden brown. You will likely need to do this in two batches. Note: The chicken will not be fully cooked yet. Set the browned chicken aside on a clean plate to rest.

To make the sauce, make sure you have all of the sauce ingredients prepped and ready, as the next steps go quickly. Place the same pan back over medium-high heat. Add 4 tablespoons (60 g) of the butter, and as soon as the butter is melted, add the garlic and shallot. Stir for 60 seconds, then add the wine, broth, salt, and xanthan gum. Stir very well, making sure to scrape the fond off the bottom of the pan, and ensuring there are no lumps of xanthan gum. Bring the mixture to a boil, and let the liquid simmer for 5 minutes to cook off the alcohol and reduce the liquid.

Add the mushrooms and chicken, including any juices on the plate, to the pan, as well as the remaining 2 tablespoons (30 g) of the butter. Note: It will seem like too many mushrooms, but keep stirring them in; they will cook down. Turn the heat down to medium, and once the mixture is boiling, let it simmer, uncovered, for 5 minutes.

For serving, garnish the chicken with the parsley and Parmesan, if using.

CHICKEN ADOBO

2 tbsp (24 g) whole peppercorns

3 tbsp (45 g) unsalted butter or avocado oil

2½–3 lbs (1.2–1.4 kg) bone-in, skin-on chicken thighs (5 to 6 pieces)

¾ cup (180 ml) low-sodium soy sauce

1 cup (240 ml) apple cider vinegar

½ cup (120 ml) low-sodium chicken broth

8 bay leaves

12 whole cloves garlic, peeled

FOR SERVING

Steamed cauliflower rice (optional)

MACROS PER SERVING

Calories: 389 | Protein: 48.5 g

Fat: 17.6 g | Net Carbs: 6.5 g

Fiber: 0.2 g | Sugar Alcohol: 0 g

Total Carbs: 6.7 g

Serves 4 people

Filipino-Inspired Chicken Adobo

Every Filipino household has its version of chicken adobo, a true Filipino comfort food. I was lucky enough to have my dear friend and fellow chef, Allen Soriano, teach me how he makes his version. I'm convinced it's one of the most delicious dishes on Earth, and now it's a staple in my house. And, while this version is inspired by the traditional dish he taught me, I've made a few untraditional changes to make it fit for a Keto lifestyle. The salty and garlicky sauce is so good, you'll want to drink it with a spoon. So, thank you, Allen, and a big shoutout to the entire #filiketo community.

Place the peppercorns in a mortar and pestle or a resealable plastic bag. Using the pestle, or a rolling pin, gently smash the peppercorns just until they crack open into larger pieces—you don't need to turn the pepper into a fine powder. Set it aside.

In a large cast-iron or nonstick skillet, melt the butter over medium-high heat, then add the chicken thighs, skin side down, to the pan. Let the skin sear for about 4 minutes, or until the skin is brown. Note: It's OK if the chicken is a very tight fit in the pan, as it will shrink while cooking. Flip the chicken over, skin side up, and then add in the soy sauce, vinegar, broth, and crushed pepper. Give everything a stir so it's well mixed, and then nestle in the bay leaves and all of the cloves of garlic—yes, 12 cloves seem crazy, but it's worth it. Heck, sometimes I put in even more!

Bring the cooking liquid back to a boil and, once it's bubbling, drop the heat to medium-low and let the mixture simmer, uncovered, for 45 minutes. Adjust the heat as needed, as you want a steady, gentle boil in the pan the entire time.

For serving, spoon some of the sauce over the top of the chicken, and serve it family-style, right out of the skillet. Serve with a side of the cauliflower rice, if using.

12 oz (340 g) sugar-free bacon, cut into 1-inch (3-cm) slices

2 lbs (910 g) chicken tenders, cut into 1-inch (3-cm) slices

½ tsp sea salt

1 tsp dried oregano

2 tsp (6 g) garlic powder

½ tsp black pepper

8 oz (230 g) broccoli, cut into florets

1 cup (240 ml) ranch dressing (see Pro Tip)

½ cup (40 g) shredded mozzarella cheese or Italian-blend cheese

---

MACROS PER SERVING

Calories: 876 | Protein: 71.1 g

Fat: 58.6 g | Net Carbs: 10.7 g

Fiber: 2.0 g | Sugar Alcohol: 0

Total Carbs: 12.7 g

Serves 4 people

Homestyle Chicken-Bacon-Ranch Skillet

Am I the only one that loved a chicken-bacon-ranch sub from Subway? Well, I turned it into a simple one-pot dinner that the whole family will enjoy. Packed with protein and healthy fat, this dinner is gooey, delicious, and perfect for a Keto lifestyle. Very kid-friendly, and quick enough for a busy weeknight, this recipe can be made in minutes and packs a big punch of flavor.

In a large nonstick or cast-iron skillet over medium heat, cook the bacon until it's all evenly cooked and crispy. This should take about 6 minutes. Remove the bacon from the pan and set it aside, but leave all the bacon grease in the pan.

Turn the heat up to high, then add the chicken, salt, oregano, garlic powder, and pepper. Stir everything well, coating the chicken in the spices, and let the chicken brown in the pan for 2 minutes. Add in the broccoli, and stir everything in the pan to coat the broccoli.

Using a large pot lid, or even a piece of aluminum foil, cover the skillet and turn the heat down to medium. Let the chicken and broccoli cook for 2 minutes, or until the broccoli is just cooked through and fork-tender, not soft. If it needs another minute or two, place the lid back on. Once the broccoli is just cooked, turn off the heat, and stir in the ranch dressing and the cheese, as well as the cooked bacon. The residual heat in the pan will melt the cheese and warm the sauce.

I like to serve this dish family-style, right out of the pan.

Pro Tip: To really step up the flavor of this dish and avoid the processed oils found in most store-bought dressings, try making your own ranch dressing, found on page 16.

10 oz (280 g) grape tomatoes, halved

2 tbsp (30 ml) olive oil

2 tbsp (30 ml) balsamic vinegar

1½ lbs (680 g) thin-sliced chicken breasts

½ tsp sea salt

¼ tsp black pepper

¾ cup (180 g) pesto (see Pro Tip)

8 oz (230 g) fresh mozzarella cheese or burrata cheese, sliced

---

MACROS PER SERVING

Calories: 576 | Protein: 48.8 g

Fat: 36.1 g | Net Carbs: 2.9 g

Fiber: 0.5 g | Sugar Alcohol: 0 g

Total Carbs: 3.4 g

Serves 4 people

Sheet Pan Pesto Chicken with Jammy Tomatoes

There's nothing quite like perfectly sweet tomatoes and basil in the summertime, and this recipe will bring you right back to a warm summer night any time of year. The bright, simple ingredients in this just sing together. This is the recipe I promise you'll be going back to week after week. It's easy enough to throw together on a weeknight, but impressive enough to serve to company. The combination of the roasted jammy tomatoes, the herbal pesto, and the gooey fresh mozzarella will have you fighting for seconds. This recipe goes really well with a nice arugula salad, topped with balsamic vinaigrette and shaved Parmesan.

Try pairing this with the Belly-Warming Baked Broccoli Alfredo (page 111).

Start by preheating your oven to 400°F (204°C). Then, for easy cleanup, line a baking sheet with aluminum foil or parchment paper.

To the baking sheet, add the tomatoes, olive oil, and balsamic, and toss everything together to coat. Spread the tomatoes to the perimeter of the pan to leave room in the center for the chicken. Place the chicken on the pan, and coat the top of the chicken and tomatoes evenly with the salt and pepper. Turn the chicken breasts over and spread out the tomatoes in all the spaces around the chicken. Spoon the pesto evenly over the top of the chicken breasts.

Then, place the pan in the oven and bake it for 20 minutes, or until the chicken reaches 165°F (74°C) on an instant-read thermometer.

Remove the pan from the oven and place mozzarella slices on the top of each piece of chicken. Bake the chicken for 5 minutes, or until the cheese is melted.

Serve the dish family-style, right off the sheet pan.

Pro Tip: Jarred pesto can be found near the spaghetti sauce in nearly every grocery store. But if you're feeling chef-y, make your own! Simply add 3 ounces (85 g) of fresh basil, ⅓ cup (80 ml) of olive oil, ¼ cup (8 g) of grated Parmesan, ¼ teaspoon sea salt, two cloves of garlic, and 2 tablespoons (20 g) of pine nuts, macadamia nuts, or walnuts to a food processor, and blend until smooth. Yum!

SEARED CHICKEN

2 lbs (910 g) chicken breasts

1 tbsp (15 ml) avocado oil

1½ tsp (9 g) kosher salt

½ tsp cumin

CHIPOTLE SAUCE

1½ cups (360 ml) heavy whipping cream (see Pro Tips)

3 tbsp (48 g) tomato paste

1 (3.5-oz [105-g]) can chipotle in adobo (see Pro Tips)

1 tsp kosher salt, divided

1 tbsp (15 ml) avocado oil

1 green bell pepper, diced

1 yellow onion, diced

½ tsp cumin

2 cloves garlic, chopped

½ cup (120 g) sour cream (see Pro Tips)

FOR SERVING

Cilantro sprigs and lime wedges (optional)

MACROS PER SERVING

Calories: 754 | Protein: 52.5 g
Fat: 53.4 g | Net Carbs: 9.1 g
Fiber: 5.1 g | Sugar Alcohol: 0 g
Total Carbs: 14.2 g

Serves 4 people

Smoky Southwest Chicken Picante

This chipotle pepper–infused dish is big and bold, and inspired by Texas flavors. Yeehaw! If you're tired of the same ole, same ole chicken dinners, this is the recipe for you. Smoky, spicy, and creamy, it's packed with flavor. And while the sauce is perfect with the chicken, you'll want to slather it on just about anything. It goes well with steak or grilled shrimp as well.

Start by pulling your chicken out of the fridge to temper for 30 minutes.

Meanwhile, start the sauce. In a blender or food processor, add the cream, tomato paste, two individual peppers from the can of chipotles, and ½ teaspoon of the salt. Pulse the ingredients a few times, just until blended. Do not overmix, or you will whip the cream.

In a large nonstick skillet, warm the avocado oil over medium-high heat. Meanwhile, season both sides of the chicken with the salt and cumin. Once the pan is smoking hot, sear the chicken for 5 minutes on each side, or until it is browned and has an internal temperature of 165°F (74°C). Remove the chicken from the pan, and set it aside on a plate to rest.

Using the same pan, turn the heat up to high, and add the avocado oil. Once hot, add the bell pepper, onion, remaining ½ teaspoon of salt, and cumin. Sauté for about 5 minutes, or until the onions are translucent. Add the garlic, and sauté for 1 more minute. Then, add in the cream mix from the blender, stirring to combine the ingredients. Once the chipotle sauce is hot and bubbly, turn off the heat, and stir in the sour cream. Place the chicken back in the pan, and spoon some of the sauce over it to coat it.

For serving, garnish the chicken with the cilantro and lime wedges, if using. You can serve it family-style, right from the pan.

Pro Tips: To make this dairy free, swap the heavy whipping cream for a 13.5-ounce (400-ml) can of unsweetened coconut cream and omit the sour cream.

Chop up the remaining chipotle peppers and mix them with mayonnaise for a delicious, spicy chipotle aioli.

YOU GOTTA *beef* WITH ME?

I mean, what's better than a juicy burger (page 41) or a perfectly cooked brisket (page 54)? Beef is so delicious and extremely nutrient-dense, so these recipes will keep you and yours fed, happy, and healthy. If you don't try all these beefy recipes, it'd be a big missed steak.

Famous French Onion Meatloaf—Upgraded!	38
Jalapeño Popper–Stuffed Burgers with "Animal Sauce"	41
Crispy Garlic Butter Steak	42
Giant Showstopping Meatballs in Rosé Sauce	45
Grilled Carne Asada with Homemade Salsa Roja	46
Philly Cheesesteak—Hold the Bun!	49
Low & Slow Texas Brisket Chili	50
A Little Fancy Steak au Poivre	53
Brisket for the Holidays	54

2 lbs (910 g) 80/20 ground beef

¼ cup (28 g) onion powder

2 tbsp (18 g) garlic powder

1 tbsp (6 g) paprika

1 tbsp (6 g) black pepper

1 tbsp (4 g) Italian herb blend

1 tbsp (10 g) beef bouillon powder

2 eggs

2 tbsp (32 g) yellow mustard

½ cup (120 g) sugar-free ketchup, divided

Nonstick cooking spray

2 tbsp (30 g) salted butter

1 yellow onion, thinly sliced

¼ tsp sea salt

¾ cup (81 g) shredded Gruyère or Swiss cheese

MACROS PER SERVING

Calories: 593 | Protein: 42.4 g

Fat: 41.5 g | Net Carbs: 10.7 g

Fiber: 1.8 g | Sugar Alcohol: 0 g

Total Carbs: 12.5 g

Pro Tip: For an even more over-the-top version, stuff the middle of the meatloaf with another ½ cup (54 g) of the Gruyère while you're packing it into the loaf pan. It's an insane stuffed meatloaf!

Serves 6 people

Famous French Onion Meatloaf—Upgraded!

Based on my viral recipe, this is Version 2.0! I know, I know, don't fix what ain't broken . . . but this version takes it to the next level—just wait until you try the caramelized onion and Gruyère topping! Easy, inexpensive, and a crowd-pleaser, this meatloaf is not the dry, boring meatloaf from the school cafeteria. This is juicy, delicious indulgence.

Try pairing this with the Garlic Parmesan Green Beans (page 112).

Preheat your oven to 400°F (204°C). To a large mixing bowl, add the beef, onion powder, garlic powder, paprika, pepper, Italian herbs, bouillon, eggs, mustard, and ¼ cup (60 g) of the ketchup.

Use your hands to knead all of the ingredients together until they are very well mixed. Tip: Use rubber gloves for easy cleanup. Grease a loaf pan with the cooking spray, and press the meatloaf into the pan.

Then, brush the top of the meatloaf with the remaining ¼ cup (60 g) of ketchup. Cover the pan with aluminum foil, cutting a vent in the top of the foil to let the steam escape. Bake the meatloaf for 50 to 60 minutes, removing the aluminum foil halfway through. Note: The exact cooking time will depend on the shape of your loaf pan, so using a thermometer is the best option for this recipe. Remove the meatloaf from the oven when the internal temperature on an instant-read or meat thermometer reads 155°F (68°C) at the center.

While the meatloaf cooks, add the butter to a skillet over medium heat. Once it's melted, add the onion and salt, and sauté for 15 to 20 minutes, or until they are soft and caramelized. If the onions start to burn, lower the heat.

When the meatloaf is done, pull it out of the oven and turn the oven to broil. Top the meatloaf with the caramelized onions. Then, top the onions with the cheese. Broil the meatloaf for 2 to 3 minutes, or until the cheese is bubbly.

Let the meatloaf rest for at least 15 minutes to ensure a juicy result. After resting, cut it into 1-inch (3-cm)-thick slices, and serve.

"ANIMAL SAUCE"

¼ cup (60 g) mayonnaise

2 tbsp (30 g) sugar-free ketchup

2 tsp (8 g) granulated sweetener

2 tbsp (33 g) dill relish

STUFFED BURGERS

6 oz (170 g) cream cheese, softened

3 tbsp (45 g) drained jarred diced jalapeño

3 tbsp (21 g) 100% bacon bits

2 lbs (910 g) 80/20 ground beef

½ tsp sea salt

¼ tsp black pepper

1 tbsp (15 ml) avocado oil

4 slices cheddar cheese

FOR SERVING

Lettuce leaves, tomato slices, and/or red onion (optional)

MACROS PER SERVING

Calories: 960 | Protein: 50.4 g

Fat: 81.6 g | Net Carbs: 1.8 g

Fiber: 0.2 g | Sugar Alcohol: 2 g

Total Carbs: 4.0 g

Jalapeño Popper-Stuffed Burgers with "Animal Sauce"

I love a perfectly cooked burger, but this recipe takes it up a notch. The jalapeño popper stuffing not only provides a burst of flavor, but it keeps the burgers incredibly juicy. And the Keto-friendly In-N-Out-inspired "Animal Sauce" will have you dreaming of it for days. In fact, I'd make a double batch of the sauce and keep the leftovers in your fridge for later. You can also grill these burgers at your next cookout.

Try pairing this with the Bacon & Bleu Coleslaw (page 119).

To make the sauce, mix together the mayo, ketchup, sweetener, and relish in a small mixing bowl, and place it in the fridge to cool. Save any extra in a lidded jar for up to 10 days.

To make the burger filling, add the cream cheese, jalapeño, and bacon bits to a small bowl, and mix well to combine.

Divide the ground beef into eight even pieces, and roll them into balls, like meatballs. Use your hands to smash each ball into a thin, flat patty about ¼ inch (6 mm) thick. Divide the filling evenly into the center of four of the patties. Then, top each patty with a second patty, and use your fingers to press and seal the meat around the filling. You can use your hands to reshape the stuffed burgers into even patties about 1 inch (3 cm) thick; just make sure you've completely sealed the two patties together. Sprinkle both sides of the burger with the salt and pepper.

Warm up the avocado oil in a large skillet or griddle over very high heat. Once the pan is smoking hot, sear the burgers for 4 minutes. Flip them, and cook them for 4 minutes on the other side, topping with the cheese slices halfway through the cooking time. Remove the burgers to a clean plate, and let them rest for 5 minutes before serving them.

For serving, wrap the burger in a lettuce leaf, if using, with a generous spread of the "Animal Sauce."

Pro Tip: For a restaurant-style upgrade, add extra toppings like sautéed onions, crispy bacon, avocado, or even a fried egg.

2 lbs (910 g) flank steak

6 tbsp (90 g) salted butter

1 sprig fresh rosemary

10 cloves garlic, chopped

2 tsp (12 g) kosher salt

2 tsp (4 g) black pepper

1 tbsp (15 ml) avocado oil

MACROS PER SERVING

Calories: 594 | Protein: 50.7 g

Fat: 41.3 g | Net Carbs: 2.8 g

Fiber: 0.4 g | Sugar Alcohol: 0 g

Total Carbs: 3.2 g

Serves 4 people

Crispy Garlic Butter Steak

The smell of garlic and butter cooking is perhaps the most comforting aroma on earth: It just reminds me of home. While this recipe may seem simple, the result is anything but. The rosemary-infused butter and the crispy garlic are absolutely addicting. You'll wonder where this has been your whole life. The crunch with the juicy steak will make this one of the best steaks you've ever made. I promise.

Try pairing this with the Cheesy Low-Carb Scalloped "Potatoes" (page 104).

Pull the steak out of the fridge 15 minutes before cooking to let it come to room temperature.

To make the crispy garlic butter, start by placing the butter in a small saucepan or frying pan over medium-low heat. As soon as it is melted and warm, add the sprig of rosemary to the pan, and gently stir the rosemary around in the butter for about 30 seconds to infuse the butter with the beautiful rosemary flavor. Add the garlic to the pan, and let the garlic cook in the butter for about 8 to 10 minutes, or until the garlic is toasted and light brown. If the garlic starts to turn dark brown, get it off the heat. Once the garlic is golden brown, turn off the heat, discard the rosemary sprig, and set the pan aside off the stove, leaving the garlic butter in the pan to stay warm while we cook the steak.

Prepare the steak by first carefully trimming off any excess fat or silverskin on the steaks.

Place a heavy-bottomed pan or cast-iron skillet over high heat. While it warms up, coat both sides of the steak with the salt and pepper. Once the skillet is smoking hot, add the oil, then place the steak in the pan, and let it sear for 4 minutes, without moving it. Flip the steak over, and cook it for 4 minutes. For a thicker flank steak (more than ½ inch [1.3 cm] thick), add an extra minute to each side. Let the steak rest on a cutting board for at least 5 minutes.

Slice the steak against the grain into thin slices. Line up the slices on a nice serving plate, and pour that crispy garlic butter over the top.

GIANT MEATBALLS

2 lbs (910 g) 80/20 ground beef (or a combination of ground beef and pork)

1 tbsp (9 g) garlic powder

1 tbsp (5 g) dried basil

½ cup (15 g) grated Parmesan cheese

1 tsp black pepper

1 tsp sea salt

3 eggs

2 tbsp (30 ml) avocado oil

HOMEMADE ROSÉ SAUCE

4 tbsp (60 g) unsalted butter, divided

1 yellow onion, chopped

4 cloves garlic, minced

2 tbsp (32 g) tomato paste

1 (28-oz [800-g]) can San Marzano tomatoes

½ tsp sea salt

2 tbsp (24 g) granulated sweetener

1 tbsp (5 g) dried basil

1 tbsp (3 g) dried oregano

½ cup (120 ml) heavy whipping cream

MACROS PER SERVING

Calories: 834 | Protein: 57.9 g

Fat: 52.8 g | Net Carbs: 12.6 g

Fiber: 3.9 g | Sugar Alcohol: 6 g

Total Carbs: 22.5 g

Serves 4 people

Giant Showstopping Meatballs in Rosé Sauce

What's more comforting than a big bowl of spaghetti and meatballs? Well, these oversized meatballs are tender, juicy, and so good that you'll forget about the pasta completely. The easy Rosé Sauce—with a splash of cream—gives this recipe its special touch.

Preheat your oven to 275°F (135°C).

For the giant meatballs, add the beef, garlic, basil, Parmesan, pepper, salt, and eggs to a bowl. Gently knead the ingredients together just until uniformly combined—do not overmix. Press the mixture flat on the bottom of the bowl to help you divide the mixture into four even parts. Then roll each of the four parts into smooth, round—giant!—meatballs.

In a large oven-safe skillet over medium-high heat, add the avocado oil. Once it's smoking hot, gently add the meatballs to the pan. Sear them for about 90 seconds, then rotate them to another side. Continue to brown the meatballs for about 60 seconds per side, until each one is entirely seared. Then, loosely cover the pan with aluminum foil, and place it in the oven. Bake the meatballs for about 25 minutes, or until the center reads 155°F (68°C) on an instant-read thermometer.

Meanwhile, make the sauce. Place a saucepan or large skillet over medium heat. Add 2 tablespoons (30 g) of the butter. Once it's melted, add the onions, and sauté them for 3 minutes. Add the garlic and tomato paste, and sauté for 30 seconds, stirring continuously. Stir in the can of tomatoes, using the spoon to break them into small pieces. Add the salt, sweetener, basil, and oregano; stir well. Once the sauce is boiling, drop the heat to low, then simmer for 15 minutes, stirring occasionally to make sure the bottom doesn't burn. Stir in the remaining 2 tablespoons (30 g) of the butter and the cream. Turn off the heat, then cover the pot with the lid to keep it warm while the meatballs finish cooking.

Once the meatballs are cooked, set them directly into the rosé sauce, discarding the oil in the meatball pan. Spoon more sauce over the top of the meatballs. Serve family-style, while the sauce is hot and bubbly.

Pro Tip: Make a fun—and cheesy—surprise. Stuff the center of each meatball with a fresh mozzarella ball—look for "bocconcini." Yum!

CARNE ASADA

2 lbs (910 g) skirt steak

¼ cup (60 ml) avocado oil

¼ cup (60 ml) freshly squeezed lime juice (about 3 limes)

¼ cup (60 ml) soy sauce or coconut aminos

1 tbsp (3 g) dried oregano

½ tsp chipotle powder or smoked paprika

½ tsp cumin

2 tbsp (2 g) packed cilantro leaves, minced

1 tsp sea salt

¼ tsp black pepper

SALSA ROJA

1 lb (455 g) tomatoes on the vine, halved

½ red onion

1 jalapeño, seeds removed for milder salsa

3 whole cloves garlic

1 tsp chicken bouillon powder or sea salt

2 tbsp (2 g) packed cilantro leaves, minced

FOR SERVING

Avocados, low-carb tortillas, lime wedges, and/or sour cream (optional)

MACROS PER SERVING

Calories: 467 | Protein: 51.9 g

Fat: 24.4 g | Net Carbs: 5.7 g

Fiber: 2.4 g | Sugar Alcohol: 0 g

Total Carbs: 8.1 g

Serves 4 people

Grilled Carne Asada with Homemade Salsa Roja

Carne asada, which means "grilled meat" in Spanish, is a staple of Mexican cuisine, especially in Northern Mexico, where it's served at nearly every large family gathering or celebration. The steak is so juicy, thanks to the bright and flavorful marinade, and I've paired it with a simple red salsa that will rival anything you can buy at the store. Note: Classic carne asada marinade contains orange juice, but to keep this recipe low-carb, I've swapped it out for a bit of sweetener. But if you aren't strict Keto, ¼ cup (60 ml) of orange juice is a wonderful addition to the marinade. ¡Buen provecho!

Make sure your skirt steak is trimmed of any excess fat or silverskin, as this will make the beef very tough. Then set the beef aside.

In a large mixing bowl, combine the avocado oil, lime juice, soy sauce, oregano, chipotle powder, cumin, cilantro, salt, and pepper, and mix the ingredients well. Coat each piece of the beef completely in the marinade, before leaving all the beef in the marinade bowl. Wrap the bowl in plastic wrap, and marinate the meat in the fridge for at least 30 minutes, and no more than 1 hour.

Make the salsa while the meat marinates. Preheat your oven to broil and make sure the oven rack is toward the top. Line a baking sheet with aluminum foil, then place the tomatoes and onion, cut side down, jalapeño, and the cloves of garlic right onto the pan. Place the veggies into the oven and let them broil for about 5 minutes, or until they become charred and burnt on the skin. Flip the veggies over and cook the other side for 5 minutes, or until they are charred. Use tongs to transfer the veggies into a food processor or blender, discarding any water on the tray.

Add the bouillon or salt to the blender. For a smooth salsa, blend on high speed. For a chunkier salsa, just pulse the processor until you reach your desired consistency. Pour the salsa into a container and let it cool completely in the fridge. Before serving, stir in the cilantro.

Once the beef is ready, warm up your grill over very high heat, getting it as hot as you can. Oil the grill grates, then grill the meat for 2 to 3 minutes on each side. If your steaks are more than ½ inch (1.3 cm) thick, add an extra minute to each side. Let the meat rest for 5 minutes, then slice it against the grain.

Serve the meat with the salsa roja, and the avocado, tortillas, lime, and sour cream, if using.

STEAK

2 tbsp (30 ml) avocado oil or butter, divided

1 yellow onion, chopped

8 oz (230 g) white mushrooms, sliced

2 tbsp (30 ml) Worcestershire sauce, divided

2 tsp (12 g) sea salt, divided

16 oz (455 g) shaved steak (see Pro Tip)

1 tsp garlic powder

1 tsp onion powder

1½ cups (325 g) shredded Swiss or provolone cheese

FOR SERVING

⅓ cup (80 g) mayonnaise

1 head romaine lettuce, leaves separated

MACROS PER SERVING

Calories: 738 | Protein: 47.7 g

Fat: 58.8 g | Net Carbs: 8.3 g

Fiber: 1.2 g | Sugar Alcohol: 0 g

Total Carbs: 9.5 g

Serves 4 people

Philly Cheesesteak—Hold the Bun!

I spent the better part of my adult life in Pennsylvania, so I know a good cheesesteak when I see one. For this low-carb take, we're going to lose the bread, and turn it into one damn good skillet. This is a go-to weeknight meal in my house, since it's so easy and so delicious, and I'm confident it'll be a staple in your house, too.

In a large cast-iron or nonstick skillet over medium heat, add half of the avocado oil. Once it's hot, add the onion, mushrooms, half of the Worcestershire sauce, and half of the salt. Sauté the mixture for about 6 minutes, or until the veggies are soft and slightly caramelized. If they start to burn, lower the heat. Then push everything in the pan tightly up against one side of the pan.

In the open space of the pan, add the remaining half of the avocado oil, Worcestershire and salt, the steak, and the garlic and onion powders. Sauté the meat, combining it with the Worcestershire and spices. As soon as the pink color is gone on the steak, which should only take about 60 to 90 seconds, combine all the ingredients in the pan.

Spread the mixture into an even layer, turn off the heat, and then top the steak and veggies with the cheese. Cover the pan with a pot lid or aluminum foil, and let the mixture rest for 5 minutes, or until the cheese melts.

To serve the most amazing Philly cheesesteak lettuce boats, spread a generous amount of the mayo onto each romaine leaf, then fill it with a scoop of cheesesteak. Just don't forget the mayo—it makes this dish sing!

Pro Tip: Look for the shaved steak, sometimes called shaved beef or shaved ribeye, at your local grocery store. Most Asian markets will also have it. If you can't find it, ground beef will work well with this recipe, or you could slice your own ribeye into very thin slices.

CHILI

2 tbsp (30 ml) avocado oil

2 lbs (910 g) brisket (flat), cut into ¾-inch (2-cm) cubes

1 yellow onion, chopped

1 jalapeño, minced

2 tbsp (16 g) chili powder

1 tsp chipotle powder (spicy) or smoked paprika (mild)

1 tbsp (9 g) garlic powder

1 tsp cumin

1 tsp sea salt

1 (6-oz [170-g]) can tomato paste

1 cup (240 ml) beef broth

2 tbsp (30 ml) balsamic vinegar

1 (14.5-oz [411-g]) can fire-roasted diced tomatoes

1 (14-oz [397-g]) can mild or hot green chiles

FOR SERVING

Shredded cheddar cheese, sour cream, sliced scallions, or sliced jalapeños (optional)

MACROS PER SERVING

Calories: 309 | Protein: 35.3 g

Fat: 10.6 g | Net Carbs: 11.8 g

Fiber: 5.8 g | Sugar Alcohol: 0 g

Total Carbs: 17.6 g

Serves 6 people

Low & Slow Texas Brisket Chili

We all love a good, comforting bowl of chili, but here in Texas, we do things differently. Here, we don't do beans in our chili. We do brisket with a ton of spice! And we cook it low and slow, so all those flavors marry, and the brisket becomes fall-apart tender. If you can't find brisket, cut chuck into small cubes instead.

Try pairing this with the Keto Cornbread (page 144).

Warm up a Dutch oven or heavy-lidded pot over high heat with the avocado oil. Once the oil is hot, add the brisket and brown it, rotating it every 60 seconds or so, until a nice crust forms. Remove the brisket to a plate.

Turn the heat down to medium, then add the onion and jalapeño, sautéing the veggies for 2 minutes. Add the chili powder, chipotle powder, garlic powder, cumin, and salt, and sauté the mixture for 1 minute, stirring continuously. Add the tomato paste, and stir for 30 seconds. Deglaze the pot with the beef broth, scraping the bottom of the pot to remove all the spices and fond. Then, add the balsamic, tomatoes, chiles, and the seared meat.

Stir to combine the ingredients, place the lid on the pot, drop the heat to low, and cook the mixture for 4 hours, or until the brisket is tender.

For serving, ladle the chili into bowls, and top it with the cheddar, if using.

Pro Tip: For a quicker version, cook this in an Instant Pot® for 2 hours under pressure. Just let it release pressure slowly for the most tender meat. You can also use the Instant Pot's slow-cook setting, or a slow cooker, to make this. Cook it on high for 4 hours or low for 8 hours. Just make sure you still sear the meat, veggies, and spices as written.

SEARED STEAK

1 lb (455 g) New York strip or ribeye (1½ inches [4 cm] thick)

1 tsp kosher salt

½ tsp black pepper

1 tbsp (15 ml) avocado oil

CREAMY PEPPERCORN SAUCE

1 tbsp (12 g) whole peppercorns

¼ cup (60 ml) brandy, cognac, or dry sherry

3 cloves garlic, smashed

½ cup (120 ml) heavy whipping cream

2 tbsp (30 g) salted butter

¼ tsp sea salt

MACROS PER SERVING

Calories: 675 | Protein: 51.1 g
Fat: 44.0 g | Net Carbs: 2.6 g
Fiber: 0.5 g | Sugar Alcohol: 0 g
Total Carbs: 3.1 g

Serves 2 people

A Little Fancy Steak au Poivre

Feeling a little fancy? Want to impress a loved one? This recipe is for you! It brings the steakhouse to your kitchen, and it's absolutely perfect for date night—or really any night of the week. What better way is there to show your family you love them than with a special dinner? Not only is this comforting meal a hug on a plate, it walks you through searing the perfect New York strip. And, the unctuous sauce finishes the juicy steak with a touch of creaminess and spice. You can also try this with a ribeye, or even a filet mignon, if you're really feeling fancy!

Try pairing this with the Garlic Parmesan Green Beans (page 112).

Start by leaving your steak out on the countertop for 30 minutes to temper.

In a mortar and pestle or resealable plastic bag, gently crack open the peppercorns, and set them aside.

When the steak is tempered, place a cast-iron skillet over high heat. While it warms up, coat all sides of the steak with the salt and pepper. Once the pan is smoking hot—look for the wisps of smoke coming off the surface—add the avocado oil, then add the steak. Without touching the steak, let it cook for 5 minutes on that side. Flip, and cook it for 5 minutes on the other side. Then, use tongs to hold the steak on its side, and sear the fat all around the edge for 30 seconds on each side. Set the steak aside on a plate to rest. If using a meat thermometer, check out "Temp Your Meats" on page 12 for the perfect temperatures.

Meanwhile, start the sauce. Turn off the stove, and carefully pour the brandy into the pan you cooked the steak in. Step back, in case the liquor ignites; be very careful, so you don't lose your eyebrows! Once the alcohol has cooked off, about 30 seconds, turn the heat back on to medium, and add the cracked peppercorns and cloves of garlic, stirring gently. Then add the cream, butter, and salt. Use a whisk to continuously stir the sauce, scraping the bottom of the pan as you go. After about 2 minutes, all of the butter should be melted, and the sauce should start to thicken. Once the sauce is thick, turn off the heat. It will continue to thicken as it cools.

You can either serve the steak whole or carve it into thin slices. Either way, make sure to pour that creamy sauce right over the top.

2 tbsp (30 ml) avocado oil

1 tbsp (18 g) kosher salt, divided

4 lbs (1.8 kg) brisket, trimmed

2 large yellow onions, cut into 1-inch (3-cm) pieces

6 cloves garlic, smashed

¼ cup (60 ml) Worcestershire sauce

1 tbsp (6 g) paprika

½ tsp black pepper

48 oz (1.4 L) low-sugar marinara

4 bay leaves

MACROS PER SERVING

Calories: 476 | Protein: 49.7 g
Fat: 24.8 g | Net Carbs: 10.1 g
Fiber: 3.9 g | Sugar Alcohol: 0 g
Total Carbs: 14 g

Serves 8 people

Brisket for the Holidays

This is the dish my mother made for every holiday, and this cozy meal is truly a piece of my family history. It's a recipe that's been passed down many generations. And, though Mom makes it without a recipe—moms just have that special touch—we worked hard together to bring you this recipe. It's also one of the most delicious dishes you'll ever eat. I'm thrilled to share it with you, and bring you a little taste of home. I hope this dish becomes a regular at your holiday table as well.

Try pairing this with the Belly-Warming Baked Broccoli Alfredo (page 111).

Preheat the oven to 300°F (149°C), and arrange a rack in the center of the oven.

In a large Dutch oven with a lid, add the avocado oil and heat it over medium-high heat. While the pot warms up, sprinkle 2 teaspoons (12 g) of the salt on both sides of the brisket. Sear the brisket in the pot for 3 minutes on each side. Remove the brisket, and set it aside on a plate.

Immediately add the onions and garlic to the pan, and sauté them for 2 minutes. Then, add the Worcestershire sauce, stirring and scraping the bottom of the pot to remove the fond. Stir in the paprika, remaining 1 teaspoon of salt, pepper, and marinara. Turn the heat off, nestle the brisket back into the pot, spooning some sauce over the top of the meat, then add the bay leaves to the sauce. Place the lid on the pot and place it in the center of the oven. Bake the brisket for 3½ hours, stirring the sauce and spooning a bit more over the meat once every hour. At the end of the 3½ hours, remove the pot from the oven, but leave the lid on and let the pot slowly cool down over another hour or two.

You can absolutely serve this dish immediately; however, I can't recommend enough that you make this the day ahead. It gets really special resting overnight in the sauce. Simply place the cooled pot in the fridge after cooking. Before serving, remove the brisket, while it's cold, from the pot, and slice it into beautiful thin slices. Then discard the bay leaves. Place the sliced brisket back into the sauce, and bring it up to a gentle boil on the stove before serving. Trust me, this extra step is worth it!

BRINGING HOME THE bacon

Baby back ribs, pulled pork, and pizza, oh my! It doesn't get much better than this. I'm going to show you just how good pork can be, even when you leave out the sugar—there is absolutely no reason why you can't fit all your favorites into your low-carb lifestyle. From BBQ to pasta, you'll be going ham on these scrumptious dishes.

The Best Damn Keto Pizza Ever!	58
Fall-Off-the-Bone Ribs with Mike's Coffee Dry Rub	61
Million-Dollar Lasagna Roll-Ups	62
Slow Cooker BBQ Pulled Pork	65
Sausage, Peppers, & Onions with Spicy Creole Aioli	66
Guilt-Free Creamy Pasta Florentine	69

PIZZA CRUST

½ cup (15 g) grated Parmesan cheese

½ cup (60 g) almond flour

½ cup (40 g) shredded mozzarella cheese

1 tbsp (9 g) garlic powder

¼ tsp sea salt

½ tsp xanthan gum

2 eggs

Nonstick cooking spray

TOPPINGS

¾ cup (180 ml) low-sugar marinara

1 cup (80 g) shredded mozzarella cheese

½ tsp garlic powder

1 tbsp (2 g) grated Parmesan cheese

½ tsp dried oregano

¼ cup (35 g) sliced pepperoni

MACROS PER SERVING

Calories: 482 | Protein: 25.9 g
Fat: 37.8 g | Net Carbs: 10 g
Fiber: 4.6 g | Sugar Alcohol: 0 g
Total Carbs: 14.6 g

Serves 2 people

The Best Damn Keto Pizza Ever!

If you ask someone what their favorite food is, there's a good chance it's pizza. And for me, pepperoni pizza is a classic! But for those of us on a Keto or gluten-free journey, good pizza is hard to come by. So, I worked really hard to create the perfect pizza, with a crispy and chewy crust that's going to make you forget it's Keto. This recipe finally has me enjoying pizza night again.

To make the crust, preheat your oven to 350°F (180°C), and arrange racks at the top of and in the middle of the oven.

In a mixing bowl, place the Parmesan, almond flour, mozzarella, garlic powder, salt, and xanthan gum. Use a fork to combine the dry ingredients, making sure there are no lumps. Then stir in the eggs, until the mixture forms a uniform dough. Lightly grease a 12-inch (31-cm) nonstick skillet with the cooking spray. Place the ball of dough in the skillet, then take a piece of wax or parchment paper and use it to press the dough evenly into the pan. I like to smooth the dough completely, but leave a little extra lip around the edge to form the crust you expect with pizza. Place the skillet in the oven on the middle rack, and bake the crust for 20 to 22 minutes, or just until it's evenly golden brown.

For the toppings, finish the pizza as soon as the crust is done. Start by spooning the marinara on top of the pizza, leaving the outer crust of the pizza without sauce. Top it with the mozzarella. Sprinkle the garlic powder, Parmesan, and oregano on top, but be sure the full pizza gets coated, including the outer crust. Top the pizza with the pepperoni, place the whole pan back in the oven on the top rack, and bake it for another 10 minutes, or until the cheese is nice and bubbly.

Cut the pizza into eight slices and serve.

Pro Tip: Zhuzh up your pizza with other toppings, like jalapeños or sliced red onions. Get fancy with fresh mozzarella and basil for a classic margherita. Or, use leftovers from the Sweet & Sour Baked BBQ Chicken (page 19) for a BBQ chicken pizza. Go wild with your favorite toppings, as long as it's not pineapple. Pineapple doesn't belong on pizza. It's just a fact.

3 tbsp (24 g) coarse black pepper

2 tbsp (16 g) ground coffee

1 tbsp (18 g) sea salt

1 tbsp (6 g) smoked paprika

1 tbsp (15 g) sugar-free ketchup

1 tbsp (16 g) yellow mustard

3–4 lbs (1.4–1.8 kg) baby back ribs

MACROS PER SERVING

Calories: 667 | Protein: 37.3 g

Fat: 54.7 g | Net Carbs: 2.9 g

Fiber: 2.3 g | Sugar Alcohol: 0 g

Total Carbs: 5.2 g

Pro Tip: Have a pellet smoker? Try smoking these instead. I find the 3-2-1 method to be the best. Smoke the ribs at 225°F (107°C) for 3 hours unwrapped, then wrapped in aluminum for 2 hours, and, finally, 1 hour unwrapped.

Serves 4 people

Fall-Off-the-Bone Ribs with Mike's Coffee Dry Rub

Growing up, my family didn't make pork at home. But once in a while, usually on summer vacation, we'd find ourselves at a BBQ restaurant, and there was nothing I craved more than baby back ribs. Now, living in Texas, I've come to appreciate a perfect dry rub on BBQ, so I created my own, with a little not-so-secret ingredient: coffee. I also recommend you try the dry rub on your next steak too! But these ribs are truly the most tender and juicy ribs I've ever had, and you can make them easily at home in your oven.

Try pairing this with the Bacon & Bleu Coleslaw (page 119).

Start by preheating your oven to 275°F (135°C). Then, make the dry rub by mixing together the pepper, coffee, salt, and paprika. Then, in a separate small bowl, combine the ketchup and mustard. Set the dry rub and the ketchup mixture aside.

Take your rack of ribs and pat them dry on all sides with paper towels. Then, remove the silverskin on the bottom side of the ribs; you may not need to do this step if the butcher has already removed it. The easiest way to do this is to use a dry paper towel to peel off the skin—the paper towel helps get a better grip.

Take a large piece of heavy-duty aluminum foil, and place the ribs on the aluminum. Then, rub the ketchup mixture evenly over all sides of the ribs. Sprinkle the dry rub evenly over the ribs, using most of the rub on the top, meatier side of the ribs, and a lighter sprinkle on the bottom. With the ribs meat side up in the center of the aluminum, fold up the aluminum, folding the edges over to ensure a tight seal. Place the entire aluminum package onto a baking sheet for stability, and place the sheet in the oven.

Bake the ribs for 3½ hours. Remove the ribs from the oven, and turn the heat up to the highest your oven will go, plus or minus 500°F (260°C). Move the oven rack to the top row. Carefully(!) open the aluminum foil, folding it off to the side to expose the top of the ribs. Place the ribs back in the oven for 15 minutes, or until the top is dark and toasted.

Remove the ribs from the oven, and let them rest for at least 10 minutes before slicing them into individual ribs. Serve them while they are hot and juicy.

2 zucchini

1 lb (455 g) mild or hot ground Italian sausage

¼ tsp sea salt

1 tbsp + 1 tsp (12 g) garlic powder, divided

1 tbsp + 1 tsp (5 g) Italian herb blend, divided

24 oz (720 ml) low-sugar marinara

8 oz (230 g) cream cheese, softened

½ cup (15 g) grated Parmesan cheese

¼ tsp black pepper

1 cup (80 g) shredded mozzarella cheese

MACROS PER SERVING

Calories: 716 | Protein: 30.7 g

Fat: 58.6 g | Net Carbs: 12.5 g

Fiber: 2.9 g | Sugar Alcohol: 0 g

Total Carbs: 15.4 g

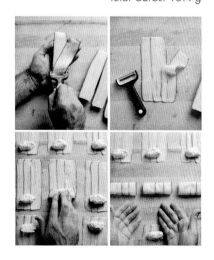

Serves 4 people

Million-Dollar Lasagna Roll-Ups

Lasagna is one of my favorite foods, so creating a Keto version was a must for me. Packed with Italian sausage and a garlic and herb cream cheese filling, this unique lasagna is elevated and beautiful. Note: If you don't eat pork, this recipe works great with ground beef or turkey.

Try pairing this with the Cheesy Garlic Breadsticks (page 143).

Preheat your oven to 375°F (190°C), and get out a 9 x 13–inch (23 x 33–cm) baking dish.

Make zucchini "planks" by cutting off the stem and root end of the zucchini. Then, slice the zucchini in half the long way, creating two long zucchini halves. Use a vegetable peeler along the open face of the zucchini to carefully shave long planks. Repeat this until you've made about 36 thin planks. With the planks, you're going to shingle together three slices for each roll-up by laying three strips lengthwise, just overlapping each other, to create twelve rectangles. Set those aside on a large cutting board.

In a saucepan over medium-high heat, brown the sausage, breaking it up into small pieces, for about 6 minutes, or until it's just barely cooked through. Then add the salt, the 1 tablespoon (9 g) of garlic powder, the 1 tablespoon (4 g) of Italian herbs, and the marinara. Stir the mixture well to combine, drop the heat to low, and let the marinara cook down for 10 minutes, uncovered.

While the marinara simmers, make the cheese filling. Add the cream cheese, Parmesan, and pepper to a small bowl, as well as the remaining garlic powder and Italian herbs. Mix well, until all the ingredients are evenly combined, and then set aside the mixture.

Assemble the lasagna roll-ups by placing a 1-tablespoon (20-g) dollop of the cheese filling on each of the twelve zucchini rectangles, dividing the cheese evenly among them. Carefully roll the zucchini with the cheese filling inside. Pour most of the meat sauce into the bottom of the baking dish, then nestle the roll-ups in the pan in two lines. Top with a bit more sauce, then the mozzarella.

Bake the roll-ups for about 20 minutes, or until the cheese on top is brown and bubbly. Let the roll-ups rest for 10 minutes before serving them.

PULLED PORK

5 lbs (2.3 kg) pork shoulder or butt

4 cups (946 ml) chicken broth

2 tbsp (30 ml) liquid smoke

½ cup (120 ml) apple cider vinegar

1 tbsp + ½ tsp (21 g) sea salt, divided

3 bay leaves

1 tsp whole peppercorns

SUGAR-FREE HICKORY BBQ SAUCE

1 (15-oz [425-g]) can tomato sauce

¼ cup (60 ml) apple cider vinegar

2 tbsp (30 ml) Worcestershire sauce

½ cup (120 g) sugar-free ketchup

1 tbsp (15 ml) hickory flavored liquid smoke

1 cup (192 g) allulose sweetener

1 tbsp (9 g) garlic powder

2 tbsp (12 g) onion powder

2 tbsp (12 g) smoked paprika

1 tsp sea salt

MACROS PER SERVING

Calories: 471 | Protein: 43.4 g
Fat: 28.9 g | Net Carbs: 5.3 g
Fiber: 1.5 g | Sugar Alcohol: 19 g
Total Carbs: 25.8 g

Pro Tip: Use a stand mixer with the whisk attachment, or an electric hand mixer, to shred your meat in seconds.

Serves 10 people

Slow Cooker BBQ Pulled Pork

Sweet, tangy, and delicious, I love a big ol' plate of pulled pork, and this sugar-free version leaves nothing to be desired. Slow cooking the pork ensures it is tender and juicy, and the homemade BBQ sauce is smoky and sweet. Just don't forget to serve it with a side of pickles. They go together so perfectly.

Try pairing this with the No Big Dill "Potato" Salad (page 108).

Using a large knife, cut the pork shoulder or butt into roughly 2-inch (5-cm) cubes; there is no need for perfection! Set the pork cubes into a slow cooker or Instant Pot. Then, add in the broth, liquid smoke, vinegar, 1 tablespoon (18 g) of the salt, bay leaves, and peppercorns. Stir the contents, then place the lid on the slow cooker. Turn on the slow cooker and cook the mixture for 4 hours on high, or 6 hours on low. If you are using an Instant Pot, set it to the "Slow Cook" function, and cook the pork for 4 hours, with the vent open.

While the pork cooks, make the BBQ sauce. In a small saucepan, combine the tomato sauce, vinegar, Worcestershire, ketchup, liquid smoke, sweetener, garlic and onion powders, paprika, and salt. Over medium heat, bring the mixture to a gentle boil. Be careful, it can splatter! So, keep a lid on the pot as much as possible. Once the sauce is boiling and all the ingredients are combined, drop the heat to medium-low, and cook the sauce for 30 minutes, stirring occasionally, with the lid cracked to let the steam escape. Turn off the heat, and let the sauce cool. It will thicken and darken in color as it cools. Store the sauce in the fridge for up to 30 days.

Once the pork is cooked, use a slotted spoon to transfer it to a large bowl, being sure not to get any bay leaves or peppercorns in the bowl. Reserve ½ cup (120 ml) of the cooking broth, then pour out and discard the remaining contents of the slow cooker.

Using two forks, shred the pork in the bowl (see Pro Tip), then add the shredded meat right back into the slow cooker. Add in the reserved broth, as well as the remaining ½ teaspoon of salt and 2 cups (480 ml) of the BBQ sauce. Stir everything well to combine the ingredients. You can serve the pork right away, or you can turn the slow cooker back on, and let it stay warm until you're ready to serve.

CREOLE AIOLI

¼ cup (60 g) mayonnaise

1 tbsp (21 g) creole or spicy brown mustard

½ tsp Cajun seasoning (I prefer Slap Ya Mama brand)

1 tsp smoked paprika

⅛–¼ tsp hot sauce

SAUSAGE SKILLET

2 tbsp (30 ml) avocado oil, divided

2 bell peppers, any color, sliced

1 large yellow onion, sliced

12 oz (340 g) andouille sausage, sliced

3 cloves garlic, chopped

2 tbsp (32 g) tomato paste

¼ cup (60 ml) low-sodium chicken broth

½ tsp dried oregano

½ tsp Cajun seasoning (I prefer Slap Ya Mama brand)

1 tsp smoked paprika

MACROS PER SERVING

Calories: 412 | Protein: 22.6 g

Fat: 28.3 g | Net Carbs: 7.6 g

Fiber: 3.4 g | Sugar Alcohol: 0 g

Total Carbs: 11 g

Serves 4 people

Sausage, Peppers, & Onions with Spicy Creole Aioli

This dish, inspired by the flavors of New Orleans, is a party on a plate—popping with big flavors and colors—and is so easy to make. Sweet, spicy, and oh-so-comforting, this one-pot dinner is a fun way to bring the heat to your table. You can even dress it up by adding some peeled shrimp. The zesty sauce is the perfect creamy complement to the savory skillet.

Try pairing this with the Cauliflower Dirty Rice (page 116).

Start by making the aioli. In a small bowl, combine the mayo, mustard, Cajun seasoning, paprika, and hot sauce, and mix well. Set the sauce aside for serving.

In a large nonstick or cast-iron skillet over high heat, add 1 tablespoon (15 ml) of the oil and, once it's smoking hot, add the bell peppers and onion, stirring them in the oil. Leave the veggies in the pan without stirring them for 1 minute at a time to build a nice char on them. Stir, and repeat for about 5 minutes, or until the veggies have nice browned edges and are just cooked through and tender. Pour the veggies onto a plate, and set it aside.

Using the same skillet, drop the heat to medium, then add the remaining 1 tablespoon (15 ml) of oil and the sausage. Sauté the mixture for 3 minutes, or just until the sausage has browned. Add the garlic and the tomato paste. Stir constantly for 1 minute, then add the chicken broth, oregano, Cajun seasoning, and paprika. Stir well to combine, then stir in the cooked peppers and onions as well.

Turn the heat off, and drizzle the aioli on top of the skillet. Serve the dish family-style, right out of the skillet.

2 tbsp (30 ml) avocado oil

1 lb (455 g) mild or hot ground Italian sausage

8 oz (230 g) cremini or white mushrooms, sliced

¼ tsp sea salt

½ tsp black pepper

½ cup (120 ml) dry white wine

2 tsp (2 g) Italian herb blend or dried basil

1 tbsp (9 g) garlic powder

½ cup (120 ml) heavy whipping cream

4 oz (113 g) cream cheese

4 oz (113 g) fresh baby spinach

¼ cup (8 g) shredded Parmesan cheese, plus more for garnish

8 oz (230 g) Palmini noodles or low-carb pasta, drained and rinsed

---

MACROS PER SERVING

Calories: 631 | Protein: 25.7 g
Fat: 47.8 g | Net Carbs: 11 g
*Fiber: 2.8 g | Sugar Alcohol: 0 g
Total Carbs: 13.8 g*

Serves 4 people

Guilt-Free Creamy Pasta Florentine

Sometimes we just need a big bowl of pasta! This recipe is so rich and creamy, it will certainly put a smile on your face. The combination of the Italian sausage with the savory mushroom sauce is heavenly. I recommend the Palmini noodles, made from hearts of palm, from Amazon, or the Healthy Noodles from Costco. If you can't find those, use your favorite low-carb pasta substitute or zucchini noodles. If you don't love pork, this recipe works great with cubed boneless chicken or chicken sausage instead.

Try pairing this with the Cheesy Garlic Breadsticks (page 143).

In a large skillet over medium-high heat, heat the avocado oil. When it's hot, add the sausage. Before breaking up the meat, let it sear for 2 minutes on each side to get a nice brown crust. Then, use a spatula or spoon to break the meat into ½-inch (1.3-cm) pieces—you don't need to break it up into a full ground meat consistency, as the bite-sized morsels of sausage are nice in the dish.

Add the mushrooms, salt, and pepper, and sauté for 2 minutes. Pour in the white wine, Italian herbs, and garlic powder, and stir, scraping the bottom of the pan to remove any fond. Sauté the mixture for 3 minutes, or until most of the liquid in the pan has evaporated.

Drop the heat to medium-low, add the cream and cream cheese, and stir continuously, breaking up the cream cheese until it's fully melted into the sauce. Then, carefully stir in the spinach. Note: It will seem like a crazy amount of spinach, but keep folding in the spinach just until it wilts into the sauce.

Fold in the Parmesan and pasta, and just when the pan is bubbly and hot, turn off the heat. Top the pasta with an extra sprinkle of Parmesan, and serve it family-style, right from the pan.

KEEPIN'
IT
reel

Growing up in Maryland, seafood was king. Some of my best memories are fishing and crabbing with my dad on the Chesapeake Bay. Those memories are very near and dear to me. These seafood recipes are rich enough to give you all the comforting feelings, but healthy enough to help keep you feeling your best. From Stunning Brown Butter Shrimp & Grits (page 76) to Crispy Fried Fish Tacos with Baja Sauce (page 75), these dishes will make you forget they're Keto. Trust me, you'll be hooked!

Garlic Lovers' Shrimp Scampi	72
Crispy Fried Fish Tacos with Baja Sauce	75
Stunning Brown Butter Shrimp & Grits	76
Sweet Teriyaki-Glazed Salmon	79
Sugarless Shrimp Pad Thai	80
Blackened Salmon in Creamy Cajun Sauce	83
Pepper-Crusted Tuna Steak with Sesame Ginger Chimichurri	84

2 lbs (910 g) jumbo shrimp, peeled, tails on, and deveined

½ tsp sea salt

¼ tsp black pepper

6 tbsp (90 g) salted butter, divided

8 cloves garlic, very finely minced

½ cup (120 ml) dry white wine

Zest of 1 lemon (cut the fruit into wedges for garnish)

¼ cup (60 ml) olive oil

2 tbsp (6 g) fresh parsley, chopped

MACROS PER SERVING

Calories: 519 | Protein: 48 g

Fat: 32.4 g | Net Carbs: 2.6 g

Fiber: 0.2 g | Sugar Alcohol: 0 g

Total Carbs: 2.8 g

Serves 4 people

Garlic Lovers' Shrimp Scampi

This Red Lobster copycat packs in the garlic. This buttery and delicious version is easy to make, which means you can have this treat any night of the week. Though, if you're cooking for a hungry crowd, you may want to double the recipe, because it will disappear very quickly off your table.

Try pairing this with the Low-Carb Cheddar Bay Biscuits (page 140).

Start by making sure your shrimp is thawed and dried off completely with paper towels. In a bowl, toss the shrimp with the salt and pepper.

Warm up a large skillet, with 2 tablespoons (30 g) of the butter in it, over high heat. Once the butter is hot, add the shrimp and cook them for 1 minute on each side. Then, remove the shrimp onto a plate, even if they aren't fully cooked, leaving any pan drippings in the pan.

Add the garlic to the same pan. Sauté it for 30 seconds, then pour in the wine, stirring and scraping the bottom of the pan to remove the fond. Bring the wine to a boil, and then let it simmer for 1 minute. Stir in the lemon zest, the remaining 4 tablespoons (60 g) of butter, olive oil, and parsley. Once the sauce is bubbly, add the shrimp back in and stir the mixture well. Let the shrimp simmer in the sauce for 1 minute, or until it's fully cooked and opaque.

Pour the shrimp and the garlic butter onto a serving plate or into small ramekins, and place the lemon wedges on the side.

BAJA SAUCE

¼ cup (60 g) mayonnaise

½ cup (120 g) sour cream

¼ cup (3 g) packed cilantro, finely chopped

2 tbsp (30 ml) freshly squeezed lime juice (about 1 lime)

1 tsp garlic powder

1 tsp hot sauce

COCONUT-CRUSTED FISH

12 oz (340 g) mahi-mahi, cod, or tilapia, thawed and cut into ¾-inch (2-cm)-wide spears

1 cup (120 g) unsweetened coconut flakes

¼ cup (18 g) pork crumbs or (8 g) grated Parmesan cheese

3 tbsp (24 g) Tajín chili-lime seasoning

2 eggs

¼ cup (60 ml) melted coconut or avocado oil

FOR SERVING

Low-carb tortillas (optional), shaved red cabbage, salsa, and sliced avocado

---

MACROS PER SERVING

Calories: 497 | Protein: 23.3 g

Fat: 39.6 g | Net Carbs: 4.6 g

Fiber: 4.3 g | Sugar Alcohol: 0 g

Total Carbs: 8.9 g

Crispy Fried Fish Tacos with Baja Sauce

#TacoTuesday just got turned up a notch! This recipe is inspired by a vacation to Baja, Mexico, that I took with my fiancé. The fresh seafood in Mexico was nothing short of sensational, and this recipe is sure to bring you right to the beach. Any mild white fish would work in this recipe, or even shrimp, so feel free to pick your favorite fish. And try not to lick up all the Baja sauce—it's that good.

To make the Baja Sauce, simply stir together the mayo, sour cream, cilantro, lime juice, garlic powder, and hot sauce in a bowl. Store the sauce in a lidded container in the fridge.

To make the fish, pat it completely dry with paper towels, and set the spears aside.

In a wide bowl, combine the coconut, pork crumbs, and chili-lime seasoning. In a smaller bowl, beat the eggs very well. Dip each fish stick in the eggs, let any excess egg drip off, then press the fish in the coconut mixture, until the piece is fully coated. Repeat until all the fish is coated.

Line a plate with paper towels. Warm up a large skillet over medium heat. Add the coconut oil, and bring it to about 325°F (163°C). You do not want the oil too hot here. If the oil is smoking, it's too hot. Gently place the fish in the oil and cook the pieces for about 1 minute on each side, or until the fish is golden brown and crispy. When it's finished, place the pieces on the prepared plate to cool.

For serving, stack the crispy fish and a drizzle of the Baja Sauce on the tortillas, if using, and top with the cabbage, salsa, and avocado. Happy Taco Tuesday!

Pro Tip: Make your own simple slaw to go with this by combining half of a small red cabbage, shaved, with ¼ cup (3 g) of cilantro, 1 minced jalapeño, 2 tablespoons (30 ml) of freshly squeezed lime juice, and 1 teaspoon of sea salt. Let it sit overnight in the fridge for the perfect crunchy bite.

1 lb (455 g) jumbo shrimp, peeled, tails on, and deveined

2 tsp (5 g) Old Bay Seasoning

½ tsp dried dill

½ tsp paprika

¼ tsp black pepper

8 tbsp (120 g) unsalted butter (see Pro Tip)

1 batch Creamy Smoked Cheddar "Grits" (page 115)

MACROS PER SERVING

Calories: 655 | Protein: 28.4 g

Fat: 56.3 g | Net Carbs: 6.2 g

Fiber: 4 g | Sugar Alcohol: 3 g

Total Carbs: 13.2 g

Serves 4 people

Stunning Brown Butter Shrimp & Grits

A true taste of the South, there isn't much as comforting or satisfying as a big bowl of shrimp and grits. But this low-carb version leaves nothing to be desired. And the browned butter gives this version an extra special touch. Prepare to fall in love.

If your shrimp is frozen, thaw it by soaking the shrimp in room temperature water for 10 minutes. Then, using paper towels, make sure your shrimp is completely dry. In a mixing bowl, add the shrimp, Old Bay, dill, paprika, and pepper. Stir well to evenly coat the shrimp in the seasonings.

In a large skillet over medium-high heat, add the butter and let it melt completely. After about 4 minutes, the butter will begin to brown. You'll know it's ready when you see little specks or dots at the bottom of the pan—the butter solids toasting—and the skillet will smell sweet and nutty. Don't walk away from the skillet, as the butter can burn. This process will take about 5 minutes total, but it depends on your stove's temperature.

As soon as the brown butter is ready, add the shrimp to the pan. Spread the shrimp into one layer, and let them cook for 90 seconds on one side, and then flip them and cook them for 60 seconds on the other side.

To serve, spoon the grits into bowls, and place the shrimp, with a generous drizzle of the brown butter, on top of the grits.

Pro Tip: Because the butter is the star of the show here, splurging on a high-quality imported grass-fed butter is worth it. It just has so much more flavor.

SALMON

4 (8-oz [230-g]) fillets skinless
Atlantic salmon

½ cup (120 ml) soy sauce or
coconut aminos

¼ cup (60 ml) apple cider vinegar

½ cup (120 ml) dry white wine

1 tsp black pepper

¾ cup (144 g) allulose sweetener

2 tbsp (20 g) peeled and chopped
fresh ginger

6 cloves garlic, chopped

2 tbsp (30 ml) avocado oil

1 tsp sesame seeds

1 scallion, thinly sliced

FOR SERVING

Cauliflower rice (optional)

MACROS PER SERVING

Calories: 625 | Protein: 46.7 g
Fat: 43 g | Net Carbs: 4.5 g
Fiber: 1.9 g | Sugar Alcohol: 36 g
Total Carbs: 42.4 g

Serves 4 people

Sweet Teriyaki-Glazed Salmon

Do you remember the chicken teriyaki from the mall food court growing up? Well, this is a healthier take on that by ditching the sweet sauce and deep-fried chicken, and substituting healthy omega-3-rich salmon and a sugar-free glaze instead. This tasty treat is the perfect balance of sweet and salty, and it's so quick and easy for a weeknight dinner the whole family will enjoy. Just make sure you use allulose here, as other sugar substitutes may crystallize in the sauce. You can also use this recipe on any fish, or even chicken.

Try pairing this with the Crack Brussels Sprouts with Honey Mustard Sauce (page 107).

Start by leaving your salmon on the counter for 20 minutes to come to room temperature.

Meanwhile, in a large bowl, whisk together the soy sauce, vinegar, white wine, pepper, allulose, ginger, and garlic. Then add the salmon to the bowl. Cover the bowl with plastic wrap, and let the fish marinate for at least 20 minutes, or up to overnight in the fridge.

In a large nonstick skillet over medium heat, add the avocado oil. Remove the salmon fillets from the marinade, and pat them dry with a paper towel. Reserve the marinade. Once the oil is hot, add the salmon to the pan and let it sauté for 2 minutes on each side, or just until it browns. Flip the salmon over one more time, and pour in the marinade. Bring the marinade to a boil, then drop the heat to low, and let the salmon simmer in the sauce for 5 minutes, or until the sauce gets thick and sticky. Just keep your eyes on the sauce to make sure it doesn't burn. Remove the fish from the heat.

For serving, top the salmon with the sesame seeds and scallions, and add a side of the cauliflower rice, if using.

PAD THAI SAUCE

¼ cup (60 g) tamarind concentrate (see Pro Tip)

¼ cup (60 g) fish sauce

3 tbsp (45 ml) freshly squeezed lime juice (about 2 limes)

½ cup (96 g) allulose sweetener

8 cloves garlic, chopped

2–3 tbsp (30–45 g) Sriracha or sambal

STIR-FRY

8 scallions

3 tbsp (45 ml) avocado oil

4 eggs

1 lb (455 g) shrimp, thawed, peeled, tails off, and deveined

16 oz (455 g) Healthy Noodles (from Costco) or shirataki noodles, rinsed

¼ cup (35 g) dry-roasted peanuts, chopped, divided

1 cup (113 g) mung bean sprouts, plus more for garnish

1 lime, cut into wedges

MACROS PER SERVING

Calories: 362 | Protein: 25.5 g
Fat: 19.4 g | Net Carbs: 11.8 g
Fiber: 7.2 g | Sugar Alcohol: 24 g
Total Carbs: 43 g

Serves 4 people

Sugarless Shrimp Pad Thai

Not much is more delicious than a big bowl of pad Thai—it's one of my favorite foods!—but it's typically made with sugar and rice noodles. I had to find a way to make this dish Keto-friendly. This version still brings all the warm and fuzzy memories of Thailand, but in a way that fits my low-carb lifestyle. Note: This dish cooks super fast, so having everything lined up and prepped ahead is key. And, if you don't love shrimp, you can swap it out for very thinly sliced chicken, beef, pork, or even tofu.

To make the sauce, in a small bowl, stir the tamarind, fish sauce, lime juice, allulose, garlic, and Sriracha until the ingredients are combined. Set the sauce aside.

To make the stir-fry, prep the scallions by removing the root ends, and then slicing the scallions into 2-inch (5-cm) pieces. Separate the white halves from the dark green ones. Then, warm up the avocado oil in a large nonstick or cast-iron pan, or wok. Once the oil is smoking hot, crack the eggs into the oil, and, without stirring them, let the eggs fry for 1 minute, then break them up using your spatula.

Pour in the pad Thai sauce, and let it boil for 3 to 4 minutes, or until it's reduced down by about half. Add the shrimp, and the white ends of the scallions, and fry them over high heat for 2 minutes. Add the noodles and half of the peanuts, and very gently toss the mixture so as not to break up the noodles. Cook the pad Thai for 1 minute, or until there is no longer any liquid in the pan, and turn off the heat. Stir in the dark green scallions and the bean sprouts.

To serve, divide the pad Thai into bowls, and top it with the remaining half of the peanuts. Garnish the bowls with bean sprouts and lime wedges.

Pro Tip: Find the tamarind concentrate at any Asian grocery store—it really makes this dish what it is, so it's worth it. But if you can't find it, swap it out for 1 tablespoon (15 ml) of soy sauce, 1 tablespoon (15 ml) of vinegar, and 1 extra tablespoon (12 g) of sweetener.

SALMON SKILLET

4 (8-oz [230-g]) fillets skinless Atlantic salmon

2 tbsp (30 ml) avocado oil

1 yellow or orange bell pepper, thinly sliced

8 oz (230 g) white mushrooms, sliced

1 cup (240 ml) heavy whipping cream

4 tbsp (64 g) cream cheese, softened

1 tbsp (9 g) garlic powder

1 tsp Cajun seasoning (I prefer Slap Ya Mama Brand)

2 tsp (4 g) smoked paprika

½ tsp black pepper

HOMEMADE BLACKENED SEASONING

1 tbsp (9 g) garlic powder

½ tsp onion powder

2 tsp (4 g) smoked paprika

1 tsp dried thyme

1 tsp black pepper

2 tsp (12 g) sea salt

¼ tsp cayenne (optional)

MACROS PER SERVING

Calories: 696 | Protein: 46.8 g

Fat: 51.3 g | Net Carbs: 10.5 g

Fiber: 4.2 g | Total Carbs: 14.7 g

Serves 4 people

Blackened Salmon in Creamy Cajun Sauce

Salmon is an amazing source of key omega-3 fatty acids, which reduce inflammation in our bodies, so I try to eat salmon quite regularly. So, I wanted to bring you a comforting salmon dish with a Southern kiss of flavor and spice. This recipe is bold and ensures that anyone will love this meal, salmon fans and skeptics alike. The blackened seasoning is punchy, and the Cajun sauce is so creamy, you'll be licking your plate clean. If you don't like salmon, this recipe also works great with any fish, shrimp, or even boneless chicken.

Try pairing this with the Cauliflower Dirty Rice (page 116).

Pull the salmon out of the fridge and let it rest on the counter for 20 minutes.

Meanwhile, make the blackened seasoning. Mix together the garlic powder, onion powder, paprika, thyme, pepper, salt, and cayenne, if using, in a small bowl.

Generously coat all four sides of the tempered salmon in the blackened seasoning. In a large cast-iron or nonstick skillet over medium-high heat, add the avocado oil. Once it's hot, place the salmon in the pan and cook it for 2 minutes without moving the fish. Flip the fish over, and repeat on the other side. Remove the salmon from the pan onto a plate.

Then, add the bell pepper to the pan and sauté it for 2 minutes. Add the mushrooms, and sauté for 60 seconds. Reduce the heat to medium, then add in the cream, cream cheese, garlic powder, Cajun seasoning, paprika and pepper. Stir until the cream cheese has melted and the sauce becomes smooth and creamy.

Nestle the salmon fillets back into the pan, drop the heat to low, and simmer the fish for 6 to 8 minutes, or until the salmon has an internal temperature of 125°F (52°C), stirring the sauce every minute or so.

Serve the salmon family-style, right out of the skillet.

SESAME GINGER CHIMICHURRI

¼ cup (3 g) packed cilantro leaves

1-inch (3-cm) "thumb" (15 g) peeled fresh ginger

1 clove garlic

3 tbsp (45 ml) apple cider vinegar

¼ cup (60 ml) sesame oil

1 tsp Dijon mustard

¼ tsp sea salt

1 tsp sesame seeds

SEARED AHI TUNA

2 tbsp (24 g) whole peppercorns

¼ tsp sea salt

10 oz (280 g) ahi tuna, thawed

2 tbsp (30 ml) avocado oil

FOR SERVING

Side salad or cauliflower rice (optional)

MACROS PER SERVING

Calories: 546 | Protein: 29 g

Fat: 47 g | Net Carbs: 1.5 g

Fiber: 0.3 g | Total Carbs: 1.8 g

Serves 2 people

Pepper-Crusted Tuna Steak with Sesame Ginger Chimichurri

Growing up, my mom would make us pepper-crusted tuna on the grill, and it's a taste of home for me. It's slightly spicy from the fresh cracked pepper, and the tuna is almost meaty. I paired it with a bright and tangy chimichurri to balance the richness of the tuna. This dinner is easy enough for any weeknight, but is also great to impress your guests at your next dinner party.

To make the chimichurri, place the cilantro, ginger, garlic, vinegar, oil, mustard, and salt in a food processor. Blend on high speed until the mixture is smooth. Spoon the mixture into a small serving bowl, stir in the sesame seeds, and set it aside.

To make the tuna, start by placing the whole peppercorns in a mortar and pestle or resealable plastic bag. Crack the peppercorns open to create a very coarse pepper—trust me, this fresh cracked pepper makes all the difference in this recipe!

Start warming up a large nonstick skillet over high heat. Meanwhile, evenly sprinkle the salt on both sides of the fish. Then, press the pepper gently into the flesh so it sticks. It seems like a lot of pepper, but use all of it to make a really nice peppercorn crust.

Add the oil to the pan, and once it's smoking hot and glistening, gently place the tuna in the pan. Cook for exactly 30 seconds, then gently flip the fish over and cook it on the other side for 30 seconds. Note: If you prefer your tuna more cooked through, add 2 minutes of cooking time per side.

Place the tuna on a cutting board and use a very sharp knife to carefully slice it into ¼-inch (6-mm) slices. Fan the slices out on a nice plate, and spoon a drizzle of chimichurri over the top.

Serve the ahi with a side salad or steamed cauliflower rice, if using.

Pro Tip: Try cooking this on your gas or charcoal grill for an extra yummy upgrade! Just cook the tuna for 1 minute on each side over very high heat.

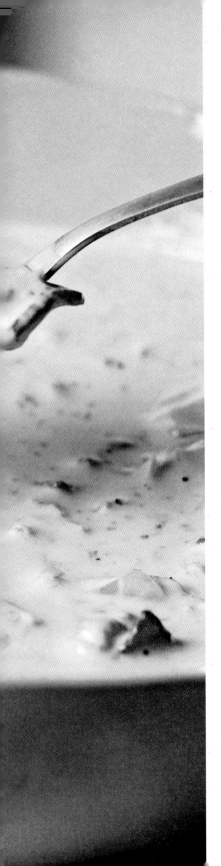

soup
FOR
THE
SOUL

Feeling the sniffles coming on, or just need something to warm you up on a chilly day? What better medicine than a big bowl of Mom's Chicken Soup (page 96)? I stewed over these recipes to make sure each one is hearty and delicious, so these low-carb bowls of goodness are sure to hit the spot. And don't think these soups are just for the side. These are complete meals, designed to keep you full and happy—without all the carbs, of course.

Cozy Loaded "Potato" Soup	88
Quick & Easy Clam Chowder	91
Bread Shop Broccoli Cheddar Soup	92
5-Hour Short Rib Beef Stew	95
Mom's Chicken Soup	96
"Hangover" Beef Pho	99
Curried Butternut Squash Bisque	100

12 oz (340 g) sugar-free bacon, cut into ½-inch (1.3-cm) pieces

1 yellow onion, diced

¾ tsp sea salt, divided

4 cloves garlic, chopped

1 cup (240 ml) chicken broth

2 cups (480 ml) heavy whipping cream

½ tsp dried sage

1 (2-lb [910-g]) head cauliflower, cut into small florets

2 tbsp (30 g) unsalted butter

½ cup (40 g) shredded cheddar cheese

¼ cup (25 g) thinly sliced scallions

MACROS PER SERVING

Calories: 570 | Protein: 31.7 g

Fat: 42.4 g | Net Carbs: 6.2 g

Fiber: 1.9 g | Total Carbs: 1.8 g

Serves 6 people

Cozy Loaded "Potato" Soup

Nothing says "comfort" more than a humble bowl of potato soup. And this version, inspired by a loaded baked potato with all the fixings—bacon, cheddar, and scallions—is simply delicious. "But wait, there's no potato in this?" Nope. I promise. This recipe is going to bring your family all the smiles, without all the heavy carbs.

Place the bacon in a cold, large soup pot. Turn the heat to medium, and fry the bacon for about 6 minutes, or until it's crispy. Once it's cooked, remove it to a plate, reserving the bacon fat in the pot.

Add the onions and ¼ teaspoon of the salt, and sauté, stirring regularly, until the onions are soft and translucent, about 4 minutes. Add the garlic, and sauté it for 1 minute. Turn the heat up to high, and add the chicken broth, cream, remaining ½ teaspoon of salt, sage, and cauliflower.

Stir well to combine the ingredients, and bring the mixture to a boil. Once it's boiling, drop the heat to medium, and cook the mixture for 5 to 10 minutes, or until the cauliflower is very soft and falling apart.

To a large blender, add the butter. Then use a ladle to carefully transfer the contents of the pot to the blender. Blend the mixture for at least 2 minutes, or until completely smooth; you may need to do this in two batches. If you have an immersion blender, you can blend the soup right in the pot, with the butter added.

When you're ready to serve, ladle the soup into bowls, and top it with the bacon, cheddar, and scallions.

6 oz (170 g) sugar-free bacon, cut into ½-inch (1.3-cm) pieces

1 yellow onion, diced

½ tsp sea salt

½ tsp black pepper

2 cloves garlic, minced

1 cauliflower stem, peeled and cut into ½-inch (1.3-cm) cubes

1 cup (240 ml) heavy whipping cream

6 oz (170 g) cream cheese

3 (6.5-oz [184-g]) cans chopped clams, divided

½ tsp Old Bay Seasoning

2 bay leaves

MACROS PER SERVING

Calories: 511 | Protein: 24.4 g

Fat: 41.2 g | Net Carbs: 6.2 g

Fiber: 1.9 g | Total Carbs: 8.1 g

Serves 4 people

Quick & Easy Clam Chowder

I suppose I should specify: This is the white version, not the red. Beyond this soup just being absolutely delicious, this is a great way to bring shellfish into your home cooking. Shellfish is incredibly good for us because it's packed with omega-3s, zinc, and B-12. And canned clams are surprisingly inexpensive; they're found near the canned tuna at your grocery store. Trust me, this soup is rich, creamy, and perfectly balanced, and you can make it in under 30 minutes. Note: This recipe uses the stem only from a cauliflower head as a low-carb swap for potatoes. So, next time you cut up a whole cauliflower, save that stem in the fridge or freezer for this recipe. You can get a stem by making the cauliflower grits recipe on page 115. If you don't have the stem, no worries! This recipe is still delicious without it. You could also add some cubed turnip, celery root, or squash, if you like.

In a saucepan or small soup pot, add the bacon pieces. Place the pan over medium heat, and fry the bacon for 6 minutes, or until it's crispy. Remove the cooked bacon onto a plate, reserving the bacon fat in the pot.

Add the onion to the pot, along with the salt and pepper. Sauté the onion for 3 minutes, then add the garlic and cauliflower stem, and cook the veggies for 3 minutes, or until the onion is soft and caramelized. Add the cream and cream cheese. Use a spoon to break the cream cheese up into smaller pieces, and gently stir the cream cheese until it is fully melted into the cream.

Then, add 1 can of the clams with the juice; drain the juice from the remaining 2 cans of clams, and add the clams and Old Bay Seasoning to the pot. Nestle the bay leaves into the soup, drop the heat to low, place the lid on the pot, and cook the chowder for 10 minutes, stirring regularly. Stir in the bacon, discard the bay leaves, and serve.

1 lb (455 g) extra sharp cheddar cheese, shredded and divided (see Pro Tip)

1 lb (455 g) broccoli (about 1 head)

2 tbsp (30 g) unsalted butter

1 yellow onion, diced

2 cloves garlic, minced

½ tsp sea salt

½ tsp black pepper

½ cup (120 ml) chicken broth

1 cup (240 ml) heavy whipping cream

⅛ tsp xanthan gum

MACROS PER SERVING

Calories: 536 | Protein: 26.5 g

Fat: 44.1 g | Net Carbs: 7.5 g

Fiber: 3.0 g | Total Carbs: 10.5 g

Pro Tip: Did you know that shredded cheese sold in bags in the grocery store is typically coated with potato starch? Not only are these hidden carbs bad for someone on Keto, but that starch can really mess up a recipe like this one. Use a food processor with the grating disk attachment to make your own shredded cheese at home in a matter of seconds.

Serves 5 people

Bread Shop Broccoli Cheddar Soup

Perhaps the ultimate comfort food, this recipe tastes just like the version from Panera Bread. But this one is better for you, since it's not thickened with a floury roux. The only thing missing here is the bread bowl! Just don't skip the extra sharp New York cheddar—all that extra flavor is key.

Measure ½ cup (40 g) of the cheddar, and reserve it to garnish the soup.

Cut the broccoli into small florets by cutting off the thick stems, but don't throw the stems away. Place all the small trimmed florets into a bowl. Take the stems, and cut them into small pieces no larger than ½-inch (1.3-cm) squares; set them aside separately from the florets.

In a large pot, melt the butter over medium heat. Once it's melted, add the onion, garlic, and cut broccoli stems, as well as the salt and pepper. Sauté, stirring occasionally, for about 5 minutes, or until the onions are soft and translucent.

Add in the chicken broth, cream, remaining cheddar, and xanthan gum at the same time. Whisk the soup continuously and vigorously for at least 2 minutes, until the cheese fully melts into the broth. Do not stop stirring it; stirring prevents the cheese from sticking or getting lumpy. As soon as the broth gets steamy, drop the temperature to low. Note: You never want this broth to boil, as this will cause the cheese to separate from the broth.

Once the broth is hot, but not boiling, stir in the broccoli florets. Stir gently, until the broth gets a bit steamy and warm but not boiling, then immediately turn off the heat. Just let the soup pot sit, stirring every minute or so, for about 5 to 7 minutes to gently finish cooking the broccoli. Once the broccoli is tender, the soup is ready to serve.

Ladle the soup into bowls, and garnish it with the reserved ½ cup (40 g) of cheddar.

You can eat this soup right away, or save it in the fridge for later, but don't reheat it in the microwave. To reheat, simply place it in a pot and slowly warm it up over medium-low heat, stirring regularly.

Ingredients

2 yellow onions, divided

2 ribs celery

3 large carrots, divided

6 cloves garlic

1 turnip, peeled

2½–3 lbs (1.2–1.4 kg) boneless beef short ribs

4 tsp (24 g) sea salt, divided

6 oz (170 g) sugar-free bacon, cut into ½-inch (1.3-cm) pieces

½ tsp black pepper

2 tbsp (32 g) tomato paste

½ cup (120 ml) balsamic vinegar

3 cups (720 ml) beef broth

3 tbsp (36 g) granulated sweetener

4 bay leaves

1 sprig fresh rosemary

MACROS PER SERVING

Calories: 667 | Protein: 49.5 g

Fat: 45.3 g | Net Carbs: 10.7 g

Fiber: 2.3 g | Sugar Alcohol: 6 g

Total Carbs: 19 g

Pro Tip: You can also make this in a slow cooker. Cook the bacon, brown the meat, and sauté the small veggies in a pan first, then add everything to the slow cooker. Cook the stew on low for 6 to 8 hours, adding the large veggies halfway through. It helps to leave the lid cracked open to let some steam escape, so the broth gets a bit thicker.

Serves 6 people

5-Hour Short Rib Beef Stew

This hearty stew is deep and complex, with a subtle sweetness from the carrots and richness from the beef short ribs. This stew can be made ahead or even frozen for later, and it's a great way to feed a crowd. If you can't find boneless short ribs, this recipe works great with chuck or stew meat.

For this recipe, I like to do all my vegetable prep work—called mise en place—first. We need to make two separate piles of vegetables: one for the sauce and one for adding to the stew later. For the sauce, finely dice one onion, the celery, and one carrot. Simply smash the cloves of garlic open. Place all of these veggies on a plate and set it aside.

Now, for the stew veggies, cut the remaining onion, remaining carrots, and the turnip into roughly 1-inch (3-cm) cubes—they don't have to be perfect—and set them aside on another plate. Finally, take the beef, and cut it into roughly 1-inch (3-cm) cubes as well, and then evenly coat the meat with 2 teaspoons (12 g) of the salt.

In a large Dutch oven or lidded pot over medium heat, fry up the bacon for about 6 minutes, or until it's crispy. Remove the bacon, leaving the grease in the pot. Turn the heat up to high. Once the bacon fat is hot, add in the beef, and let it brown for about 6 minutes total, flipping the beef over every 2 minutes, until all sides have some color. Remove the beef from the pan with a slotted spoon or tongs, and put the cubes on a plate.

Next, add your finely diced veggies, smashed garlic cloves, and pepper. Sauté the veggies for 5 minutes, or until the onions are slightly caramelized. Add in the tomato paste, and sauté the mixture for 1 minute. Then, pour in the balsamic vinegar and beef broth. Stir the bottom of the pan to remove the fond, add in the beef cubes, sweetener, bay leaf, rosemary sprig, and remaining 2 teaspoons (12 g) of salt. Gently stir to combine the ingredients. Turn the heat down to low, cover the pot, leaving the lid cracked open, and let the stew cook for 2½ hours. Note: Check on the stew and make sure it's not aggressively boiling. You want very gentle bubbles simmering, but never a full boil. Adjust the heat accordingly.

After the 2½ hours, remove the rosemary sprig and give the stew a stir, making sure nothing is sticking to the bottom, then add the large-cut stew vegetables. Cover the pot fully and cook for another 2½ hours over low heat. Again, make sure you see gentle bubbles but never a full boil. Turn off the heat, and let the stew rest for 30 minutes. It will thicken as it cools.

Serve the stew in bowls with all the tender beef and veggies you can fit.

5 lbs (2.3 kg) whole chicken or chicken quarters (see Pro Tip)

3 whole yellow onions

4 large carrots, cut into 3-inch (8-cm) pieces

4 ribs celery, cut into 3-inch (8-cm) pieces

10 cups (2.4 L) cold water

1 tsp sea salt

2 cloves garlic, chopped

½ tsp black pepper

1 tsp dried dill

2 tsp (2 g) dried parsley

3 tbsp (32 g) chicken bouillon powder

MACROS PER SERVING

Calories: 541 | Protein: 44.8 g

Fat: 35.5 g | Net Carbs: 5 g

Fiber: 1.4 g | Total Carbs: 6.4 g

Serves 8 people

Mom's Chicken Soup

My mom made this soup for every holiday, and it still remains, in my mind, the most perfect bowl of food on earth. And, fortunately for all of us, she flew to Texas to help me develop this Keto-friendly version for the book, so that it tastes just like hers. And though nothing will ever be as good as my Mom's chicken soup . . . this will get you pretty darn close.

In a very large soup pot, add the chicken, onions, carrots, and celery. Top them with the cold water and salt, and place the pot over high heat. Once the water comes to a gentle boil, simmer the mixture for 15 minutes. Drop the heat to low and use a ladle to skim off the white foam from the top. This ensures a beautiful, clear broth in the end. Stir in the garlic, pepper, dill, parsley, and bouillon. Place the lid on the pot and let the soup cook over low heat for 2 hours.

Once the soup is cooked, you'll need to strain it to remove any skin and loose bones. Take another large pot, lined with a colander, and carefully pour the soup through the colander. Use tongs to pull the carrots, celery, and onions out of the colander, and add them back into the broth. Once the chicken is cooled down enough to touch, shred the meat carefully, ensuring you don't get any bones mixed in with the pulled meat, and add the meat back into the soup. Discard the skin and bones.

Bring the soup to a simmer over medium heat, and serve. This soup can be stored in the fridge for up to 3 days and reheated before serving.

Pro Tip: The key to a good broth is having lots of bones, so you want to either cut up a whole chicken into two halves, or use chicken quarters on the bone. For an even better broth, save all your chicken bones—cooked or raw—for a few weeks or months in the freezer. When you have enough saved up, include them in this broth. You can also ask your butcher if they have any bones to buy. The more bones you can add into this broth, the better!

PHO BROTH

2 yellow onions, halved

1 large carrot, chopped

2 cloves garlic

1-inch (3-cm) "thumb" (15 g) peeled fresh ginger, sliced

8 cups (1.9 L) beef broth

2 tsp (10 g) fish sauce

3 tbsp (36 g) granulated sweetener

2 cinnamon sticks

3 star anise pods

½ tsp whole cloves

1 tsp black pepper

1 tsp sea salt

3 lbs (1.4 kg) beef bones (see Pro Tip)

TOPPINGS

16 oz (455 g) Healthy Noodles (from Costco), shirataki noodles, or zoodles

¾ lb (340 g) thinly-shaved beef

1 cup (113 g) mung bean sprouts

½ cup (6 g) loosely packed Thai basil or cilantro leaves

1 jalapeño, sliced

2 tsp (10 g) Sriracha sauce (optional)

MACROS PER SERVING

Calories: 326 | Protein: 45.3 g

Fat: 31.5 g | Net Carbs: 8.8 g

Fiber: 5.8 g | Total Carbs: 23.6 g

Serves 4 people

"Hangover" Beef Pho

Good pho is truly a culinary masterpiece. Typically, it takes several days just to make the broth, and it's a serious labor of love. But for most of us at home, making authentic pho broth is a challenge. So, I call this Keto-friendly version "hangover" pho for two reasons. First—and I probably shouldn't be sharing this, but—in college, I discovered that there was no better cure for a nasty hanger than a big bowl of pho. Second, this pho recipe is so quick and easy, you can make it right when you need it, even when you're not feeling your best. The key here is asking your butcher for beef bones (see Pro Tip below). When you find them, get a bunch and leave them in your freezer, as they are super inexpensive. If you are in serious need of a pick-me-up, this recipe is for you.

To make the broth, place the onions, carrot, garlic, ginger, beef broth, fish sauce, sweetener, cinnamon sticks, star anise, cloves, pepper, salt, and bones in an Instant Pot. Cook them for 45 minutes on high pressure. If you don't have an Instant Pot or pressure cooker, cook the mixture in a lidded pot for 3 hours over medium-low heat.

At the end of the cooking time, release the pressure. Strain and reserve the broth, using a colander or mesh strainer; discard the rest of the ingredients. Let the broth settle for a moment after straining, then take a ladle, and carefully skim off and discard the fat on the surface of the soup.

When you're ready to serve, place your cleaned broth on the stove over medium heat. While it comes to a boil, about 10 minutes, prepare the toppings in your serving bowls. I typically start with noodles at the bottom; be sure to aggressively rinse the Healthy Noodles under water first, to remove any odor. Then, add a little of the raw beef, and decorate the top with the bean sprouts, basil, and jalapeño. Just before serving, pour the boiling hot broth right over the top of the raw beef to cook it, for the perfect bite. If you like it extra spicy, like I do, add ½ teaspoon of Sriracha to each bowl, too, just before serving.

Pro Tip: Ask the butcher at your supermarket or Asian market for the beef bones. They are usually very inexpensive and really provide an authentic and rich beef flavor to the broth. If you can't find them, you can use oxtails, or simply leave out the bones and add beef bouillon powder to the broth for extra flavor.

SOUP

2 lbs (910 g) cubed butternut
squash

2 tbsp (30 ml) avocado or olive oil

½ tsp sea salt, divided

1½ cups (360 ml) vegetable or
chicken broth, plus more if needed

1 cup (240 ml) heavy whipping
cream

2 tsp (4 g) curry powder

¼ tsp ginger powder

1 tsp paprika

⅛ tsp cinnamon

DRIZZLE

¼ cup (60 g) sour cream or plain
Greek yogurt

1 tbsp (15 ml) warm water

¼ tsp black pepper

MACROS PER SERVING

Calories: 339 | Protein: 10.2 g

Fat: 23.2 g | Net Carbs: 18 g

Fiber: 3.9 g | Total Carbs: 21.9 g

Serves 4 people

Curried Butternut Squash Bisque

This warm and comforting soup really reminds me of autumn and is perfect for a chilly day at home. The recipe uses some subtle curry spice, sure to warm you up, and a sour cream drizzle to make this vegetarian soup extra rich and creamy. And roasting the butternut squash first really brings out a deeper flavor and natural sweetness that can't be beat. Typically, peeling and cutting whole butternut squash is a huge pain in the butt, so in this recipe we'll use bags of precut squash from the produce section at your grocery store. You can also make this soup ahead, and reheat it as needed. To make the soup dairy-free or vegan, swap the heavy whipping cream for unsweetened coconut cream, and drizzle the soup with good-quality olive oil, instead of the sour cream mixture.

For the soup, arrange a rack in the center of your oven, and preheat it to 375°F (190°C). Line a baking sheet with parchment paper for easy cleanup. On the baking sheet, stir the squash, oil, and ¼ teaspoon of the salt very well to ensure an even coating of oil and salt on the squash. Spread out the squash into one even layer, then bake it on the center rack for 30 to 40 minutes, or until the squash is completely soft.

As soon as the squash is done, scoop it directly into a blender. Add the remaining ¼ teaspoon of salt, broth, cream, curry powder, ginger, paprika, and cinnamon. Blend on high speed for about 2 minutes, or until the soup is totally smooth. If you find the soup too thick, you can add a little extra broth, as needed. Serve the soup right away, while it's still hot. This soup can also be refrigerated for up to 7 days and reheated in a pot.

To make the drizzle, add the sour cream and warm water to a small bowl and mix them well to combine. This will thin the sour cream, so that you can drizzle it on top of each serving of soup. Then, top each bowl with the black pepper. Note: If you make the soup ahead and refrigerate it, prepare the drizzle just before serving the reheated soup.

Pro Tip: If you want to add a little extra protein, try topping the butternut bisque with some sautéed chorizo for a complete dinner. You can find pork, beef, or even soy chorizo in your supermarket refrigerated section near the breakfast sausage.

EAT YOUR veggies!

. . . Said every mom ever. Well, believe it or not, these side dishes are going to be the star of your next meal. Heck, even your kids will love a few of these disguised veggie dishes, like the grits (page 115) or the dirty rice (page 116)! And, believe it or not, I've found a way to make veggies feel indulgent, even on a low-carb diet. Just try the Belly-Warming Baked Broccoli Alfredo (page 111) or the Cheesy Low-Carb Scalloped "Potatoes" (page 104). Make these sides with dinner, or make a few of them for your next cookout! Your guests will be begging you for the recipe. And, it's time I finally apologize for the corny puns in this book.

Cheesy Low-Carb Scalloped "Potatoes"   104

Crack Brussels Sprouts with Honey Mustard Sauce   107

No Big Dill "Potato" Salad   108

Belly-Warming Baked Broccoli Alfredo   111

Garlic Parmesan Green Beans   112

Creamy Smoked Cheddar "Grits"   115

Cauliflower Dirty Rice   116

Bacon & Bleu Coleslaw   119

2 lbs (910 g) kohlrabi or rutabaga

1 small yellow onion, chopped

3 cloves garlic

1 tsp sea salt

8 oz (230 g) cream cheese, softened

2 cups (480 ml) heavy whipping cream

2 cups (160 g) shredded cheddar cheese, divided

¼ cup (7 g) grated Parmesan cheese

MACROS PER SERVING

Calories: 380 | Protein: 15.9 g
Fat: 31.1 g | Net Carbs: 5.3 g
Fiber: 3.8 g | Total Carbs: 9.1 g

Serves 9 people

Cheesy Low-Carb Scalloped "Potatoes"

My mom used to make scalloped potatoes, and it was a favorite of mine. But this low-carb version uses a surprising substitute for the potatoes: kohlrabi. You can find it at almost any grocery store. If not, rutabaga or even turnips work, too. This is so good that your dinner guests won't even know there's no potato—you'll just have to try it to believe me.

Try pairing this with the Famous French Onion Meatloaf—Upgraded! (page 38).

Preheat your oven to 375°F (190°C). Peel your kohlrabi with a vegetable peeler. Very thinly slice the kohlrabi: Think like potato chips. I recommend doing this with a mandoline slicer, if you have one. You can also do this by hand; just take your time to get thin, even slices. Set the kohlrabi aside.

Add the onion, garlic, salt, and cream cheese to a food processor, and blend the ingredients on high speed until the mixture is smooth. Then, add the cream and blend for 10 seconds, or until the mixture is smooth.

In a medium (9 x 9–inch [23 x 23–cm]) broiler-safe baking pan or casserole dish, spread out one-third of the kohlrabi slices in one even layer—almost like roof shingles—overlapping them as you go. Pour one-third of the cream mixture on top, and sprinkle it with ½ cup (40 g) of the shredded cheese. Repeat the process again, eventually layering the ingredients three times. Top the dish with the remaining cheddar and the Parmesan. Cover the pan tightly with aluminum foil, and bake it for 1 hour. Remove the foil, and bake the casserole, uncovered, for 30 minutes.

Switch the oven to broil, and broil the casserole for 5 minutes, or until the top gets browned. Serve the dish family-style, while it's hot and bubbly.

HONEY MUSTARD SAUCE

½ cup (120 g) mayonnaise

¼ cup (48 g) granulated sweetener

1 tbsp (3 g) dried dill

2 tbsp (18 g) garlic powder

1 tbsp (15 g) Dijon mustard

2 tbsp (30 ml) freshly squeezed lemon juice

¼ tsp sea salt

SPROUTS

1 lb (455 g) Brussels sprouts, halved

MACROS PER SERVING

Calories: 214 | Protein: 1.5 g
Fat: 20.2 g | Net Carbs: 4.9 g
Fiber: 1.3 g | Sugar Alcohol: 12 g
Total Carbs: 18.2 g

Serves 4 people

Crack Brussels Sprouts with Honey Mustard Sauce

As a kid, Brussels sprouts were those soggy, smelly veggies no one really wanted. But not anymore. These little sprouts have grown up! This recipe may seem simple, but OMG . . . sweet, salty, crispy perfection. And the air fryer makes this recipe particularly easy and healthy. Just don't forget to dip the Brussels in the Honey Mustard Sauce, for that extra wow factor.

Try pairing these with the Crispy Garlic Butter Steak (page 42).

In a large mixing bowl, combine the mayo, sweetener, dill, garlic powder, Dijon, lemon juice, and salt. Mix them together well to form the sauce. Pour half of the sauce into a small dipping bowl, and set it aside for serving.

Then, stir the Brussels into the sauce remaining in the mixing bowl. Mix well, to completely and evenly coat the Brussels in the sauce.

Preheat your air fryer to 400°F (204°C). Lay out your Brussels in one even layer on the air fryer tray, and air fry them for 10 minutes, or until they are caramelized and crispy. If you don't have an air fryer, you can make these in your oven. Preheat your oven to broil, and roast the Brussels on a sheet tray on the upper rack of the oven for about 10 to 15 minutes, or until crispy.

Serve the sprouts while they are hot and fresh, with the dipping sauce on the side.

1½ lbs (680 g) celery root, also called celeriac

1 tbsp (18 g) sea salt

½ cup (120 g) mayonnaise

2 tbsp (30 g) dill relish

½ tsp dried dill

1 tbsp (15 g) Dijon mustard

¼ tsp black pepper

½ tsp lemon pepper seasoning

1 tsp granulated sweetener

MACROS PER SERVING

Calories: 170 | Protein: 1.8 g
Fat: 13.8 g | Net Carbs: 8.5 g
Fiber: 2.2 g | Sugar Alcohol: 4 g
Total Carbs: 14.7 g

Serves 6 people

No Big Dill "Potato" Salad

I have so many wonderful memories of summer cookouts with friends and family, when we would grill out in the backyard and have a spread of side dishes to boot. And potato salad is always a crowd favorite, so I had to find a way to make it healthier. And the extra punch of the dill relish provides a special touch. Just make sure to check the label when you're buying the dill relish, so you don't accidentally buy the sweet stuff. This "potato" salad uses celery root instead of potatoes for the perfect low-carb substitute. Find celery root at Whole Foods or most Asian supermarkets, or use turnips, radishes, or cauliflower instead.

Try pairing this with the Jalapeño Popper–Stuffed Burgers with "Animal Sauce" (page 41).

Bring 8 cups (1.9 L) of water to a boil in a large pot. While that heats up, prepare the celery root by peeling the rough skin off with a sharp knife. Then cut the peeled root into ½-inch (1.3-cm) cubes. Once the water is boiling, stir in the sea salt and the celery root. Boil the celery root for 8 to 10 minutes, or until it is fork tender.

While the celery root boils, prepare an ice bath in a large mixing bowl by filling the bowl with ice and water. When the celery root is tender, drain it in a colander, and immediately drop it into the ice bath to stop the cooking process and cool down the celery root. After a minute in the ice, drain the celery root again in the colander, then pat it dry with paper towels.

In a large mixing bowl, combine the mayo, dill relish, dill, mustard, pepper, lemon pepper, and sweetener. Mix well, then toss everything in with the celery root. Refrigerate the salad in an airtight container for at least 2 hours to marinate the celery root with the dressing. For best results, make this a day ahead, so the celery root can marinate for a day.

Pro Tip: Looking for a meatier version? Turn this side into a meal. Swap out the celery root for cooked cubed or pulled chicken breast for a fantastic dill chicken salad. This is also a great way to use up the meat from a supermarket rotisserie chicken.

2 tbsp (30 g) salted butter

6 cloves garlic, minced

½ tsp black pepper

2 cups (480 ml) heavy whipping cream

4 oz (113 g) cream cheese

1 cup + 2 tbsp (34 g) grated Parmesan cheese, divided

¼ cup (20 g) shredded mozzarella cheese

½ tsp Italian herb blend

1 lb (455 g) broccoli, cut into large florets

MACROS PER SERVING

Calories: 289 | Protein: 6.7 g

Fat: 26.9 g | Net Carbs: 5.9 g

Fiber: 2.1 g | Total Carbs: 8 g

Serves 6 people

Belly-Warming Baked Broccoli Alfredo

The days of boring steamed broccoli are over. This recipe brings broccoli center stage, and adults and kids alike will love this deluxe dish. Make sure you add this to the menu for your next holiday spread—everyone will be licking their plate clean. Not a fan of broccoli? You can try this with cauliflower, green beans, Brussels sprouts, or asparagus, too.

Try pairing this with the A Little Fancy Steak au Poivre (page 53).

Start by preheating your oven to 450°F (232°C). To a small saucepan over medium-high heat, add the butter. Once it's melted, add the garlic and pepper, and sauté it for 1 minute. Then, add the cream, cream cheese, 1 cup (30 g) of the Parmesan, mozzarella, and Italian herbs. Stir the mixture continuously for about 5 minutes, or until all of the cheese is fully melted and the sauce is smooth, and then turn off the heat.

Add the broccoli to a 9 x 9–inch (23 x 23–cm) baking dish. Pour the alfredo sauce over the top of the broccoli, and then toss the broccoli until it's fully coated in the sauce. Top the dish with the remaining 2 tablespoons (4 g) of Parmesan, and bake the casserole for 20 minutes, or until the broccoli is tender.

Serve the dish family-style, while it's hot and bubbly.

Pro Tip: Turn this into a bonus dinner recipe by stirring in 1 pound (455 g) of raw diced boneless chicken when you add the broccoli to the baking dish. Cook the casserole for 30 minutes, or until the chicken is cooked through.

½ lb (230 g) green beans
(see Pro Tips)

1 tbsp (15 ml) avocado oil

⅛ tsp sea salt

3 cloves garlic

1 tbsp (15 g) salted butter

¼ cup (20 g) shredded Parmesan
cheese

Freshly squeezed lemon juice

MACROS PER SERVING

Calories: 185 | Protein: 3.6 g

Fat: 14.9 g | Net Carbs: 5.8 g

Fiber: 4.1 g | Total Carbs: 9.9 g

Pro Tips: Upgrade this dish by using fresh haricots verts, or French beans. They cost a bit extra, but they don't need to be trimmed, and just look absolutely beautiful.

You can use this recipe for asparagus as well!

Serves 2 people

Garlic Parmesan Green Beans

These easy green beans come together in minutes. Packed with garlic, crisped in the air fryer, and finished with a squeeze of fresh lemon juice, these are not the soggy green beans you're used to from the can. These green beans are a showstopper, and they pair extremely well with nearly any dinner in this book. But be warned: these are so delicious, you may want to make a double batch next time.

Try pairing this with the Famous French Onion Meat Loaf—Upgraded! (page 38).

Start by trimming off the woody stem end of the green beans. Then, in a large microwave-safe mixing bowl, add the green beans, oil, and salt. Toss the mixture well until everything is evenly coated.

Preheat your air fryer to 400°F (204°C); see below for non–air fryer instructions. When the air fryer is preheated, add the green bean mixture to the tray, and cook it for 12 minutes, rotating the beans halfway through the cooking time.

While the green beans cook, use a Microplane or small grater to make a paste with the garlic cloves. Add the garlic paste to the mixing bowl you used for the beans, along with the butter. Microwave the garlic mixture for 30 seconds, stir it, then microwave it for another 30 seconds, to melt the butter and lightly cook the garlic.

Once the green beans are done, add them to the mixing bowl with the garlic butter, tossing the green beans so they get fully coated in the garlic butter. Put the beans back into the air fryer tray, top them with the Parmesan, and cook them for 1 minute, to melt the cheese slightly. Place the green beans on a large plate, and finish them with the lemon juice.

If you don't have an air fryer, you can broil the beans on the top rack of the oven for 10 minutes, rotating them as they get nice and charred. Once they are finished, toss them in the melted garlic butter and continue with the directions above.

GRITS

1 (2-lb [910-g]) head cauliflower

8 tbsp (120 g) unsalted butter

½ tsp sea salt

½ tsp white pepper

1 tbsp (12 g) granulated sweetener

¾ cup (180 ml) heavy whipping cream

8 oz (230 g) smoked cheddar cheese, shredded

FOR SERVING

½ tbsp (8 g) salted butter (optional)

MACROS PER SERVING

Calories: 374 | Protein: 12.9 g

Fat: 33.2 g | Net Carbs: 6.1 g

Fiber: 3.8 g | Sugar Alcohol: 3 g

Total Carbs: 12.9 g

Creamy Smoked Cheddar "Grits"

These yummy grits are so good, you'll forget they're not made with corn. This low-carb version is rich, creamy, and oh-so-delicious. The key to this recipe is using fresh cauliflower, not frozen, which gives it that classic grits texture. If you're tired of the usual cauliflower mash, try this instead. Also, the smoked cheddar in this recipe is the secret ingredient, so don't skip it! I get a block of it from the deli section of the supermarket and shred it at home. If you can't find it, smoked gouda is another great choice.

Start by removing the stem and leaves of the cauliflower head. Don't throw away the stem; try using it in the Quick & Easy Clam Chowder on page 91. Cut the cauliflower into small florets. In a food processor, add one-third of the cauliflower florets. Process the florets on high speed, until they are uniformly minced. Remove the minced cauliflower and place it in a bowl. Repeat the process two more times, until all of the cauliflower is processed.

In a large saucepan over medium heat, melt the butter. Once it's melted, add in the cauliflower, and stir it for 2 minutes as the cauliflower gently sautés. Drop the heat to medium-low, then add the salt, pepper, sweetener, cream, and cheddar; stir continuously for 4 minutes, or until the cauliflower is cooked and the grits start to thicken. Note: For this recipe, you want the cauliflower to be al dente, mostly cooked through, but slightly toothsome, to give it that classic grits texture.

Remove the pan from the heat, and let the grits rest for 5 minutes to continue thickening, stirring once again before serving.

Serve the grits with a pat of the butter, if using, on top.

1 tbsp (15 ml) avocado oil

2 tbsp (30 g) unsalted butter, divided

1 yellow onion, chopped

1 green bell pepper, diced

2 ribs celery, chopped

1 tbsp (16 g) tomato paste

1 lb (455 g) ground sausage or beef

½ tsp sea salt

1 tbsp (9 g) garlic powder

1 tsp black pepper

1½ tbsp (7 g) paprika

2 tsp (8 g) Cajun seasoning (I prefer Slap Ya Mama brand)

14 oz (400 g) fresh, not frozen, cauliflower rice

MACROS PER SERVING

Calories: 338 | Protein: 15.9 g
Fat: 26.7 g | Net Carbs: 8.2 g
Fiber: 3.3 g | Total Carbs: 11.5 g

Serves 6 people

Cauliflower Dirty Rice

I was first introduced to Southern dirty rice by my fiancé when visiting their North Carolina home. And I immediately fell in love. The seasoned rice with the ground meat was perfect! So, I had to make a Keto-friendly version. One thing you'll learn about me is that I don't like cauliflower rice. But this recipe is the exception to that rule. The bold flavors and meaty ingredients make this cauli rice a winner. It's full of meat and veggies for a fantastic protein-packed side, but it can also be served as a main course if you'd like.

Try pairing this with the Smoky Southwest Chicken Picante (page 35).

In a large cast-iron or nonstick skillet over medium-high heat, add the avocado oil and 1 tablespoon (15 g) of the butter. Once it's melted, add the onion, bell pepper, and celery. Sauté for about 3 minutes, or just until the veggies are slightly browned, but not cooked through. Add the tomato paste, and stir well for 30 seconds to combine it.

Move the veggies up against one side of the pan, and add the sausage to the open space. Smash the meat into one layer on the pan, but do not break it up yet. Let the meat sear on one side for about 2 minutes, or until it forms a dark brown crust, then flip it over and repeat; it's almost like a giant burger patty. Once both sides have fully browned, chop up the meat into small pieces, and stir it in with the veggies. Let it cook for 2 minutes.

Add in the salt, garlic powder, pepper, paprika, Cajun seasoning, and cauli rice. Stir well to fully combine the ingredients, and cook the rice for 3 to 4 minutes, or until nearly all of the liquid has evaporated, stirring regularly. Make sure the cauliflower isn't completely soft, as it will continue cooking after you remove the dish from the heat. Turn off the heat, and stir in the remaining tablespoon (15 g) of butter, to coat the rice and make it extra rich and delicious.

Pour the dirty rice into a large serving bowl, and serve it while it's steaming hot.

6 oz (170 g) sugar-free bacon, cut into ½-inch (1.3-cm) pieces

½ small shallot, finely minced

1 tbsp (15 g) Dijon mustard

2 tbsp (30 ml) white wine vinegar

1 tbsp (12 g) granulated sweetener

⅛ tsp sea salt

⅛ tsp black pepper

⅓ cup (80 g) mayonnaise

12-oz (340-g) bag coleslaw mix or shaved cabbage (see Pro Tips)

½ cup (60 g) crumbled bleu cheese (see Pro Tips)

MACROS PER SERVING

Calories: 272 | Protein: 13.6 g

Fat: 21.3 g | Net Carbs: 2.3 g

Fiber: 1.5 g | Sugar Alcohol: 3 g

Total Carbs: 6.8 g

Serves 6 people

Bacon & Bleu Coleslaw

I think it's time that coleslaw had its moment in the spotlight. This coleslaw is definitely ready to party. The smoky bacon with the creamy bleu cheese really makes this slaw shine. Serve it at your next cookout, or put it on top of your next burger. And if you don't like bleu cheese, don't worry. The Pro Tips below have some great options for you.

Try pairing this with the Fall-Off-the-Bone Ribs with Mike's Coffee Dry Rub (page 61).

In a skillet, fry the bacon over medium heat until it's crispy, about 6 minutes total. Once it's cooked, set the bacon aside on a cutting board, and remove the pan from the heat to cool; do not discard the bacon grease.

In a large mixing bowl, whisk together the shallot, mustard, vinegar, sweetener, salt, and pepper. Then, very slowly drizzle in a little bit of the bacon grease. Whisk aggressively and continuously, as you drizzle in more bacon fat, a little at a time, until you've used it all. Whisk until the dressing comes together (emulsifies), then add in the mayo, and mix it in.

Add the coleslaw mix to the bowl, and toss well to coat the mix in the dressing. Then add the bacon pieces and bleu cheese. Gently toss the coleslaw one more time, then cover the bowl with plastic wrap, and let the slaw marinate in the fridge for at least 30 to 60 minutes before serving it.

Pro Tips: Don't like bleu cheese? Swap it for shaved Parmesan or crumbled goat cheese instead.

Want to impress your dinner guests? Try making this with shaved Brussels sprouts instead of cabbage for an elevated twist on a classic.

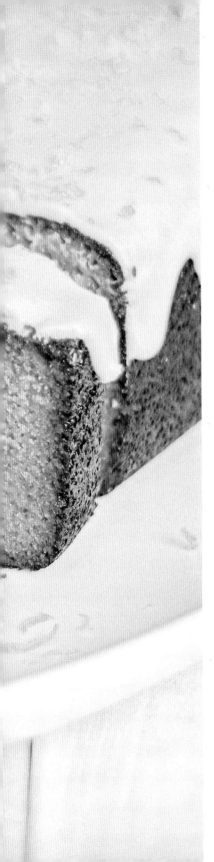

A LITTLE SOMETHIN' sweet

Would a comfort food book even be a comfort food book without dessert? Spoiler alert: The answer is "no." This collection of treats is a perfect way to get in that sweet bite without all the sugars and carbs. Finally, you can have your cake, and eat it too! Seriously, try the coconut cake on page 134. I promise you, these recipes are the jam, whether you're Keto or not. And, while most of these desserts are big enough to share, I understand if you want them all to yourself. No judgment here.

Ooey Gooey Double Chocolate Brownies	122
Cinnamon Roll Cheesecake Bites	125
Lemon Pound Cake with Lemony Cream Cheese Glaze	126
Velvety Peanut Butter Cup Mousse with Homemade Chocolate Sauce	129
No-Churn Mint Chocolate Chip Ice Cream	130
Triple Berry Crisp	133
Coconut Cake with Coconut Cream Cheese Frosting	134
Magical Strawberry Icebox Pie	137

1 cup (80 g) unsweetened cocoa powder, plus 1 tbsp (5 g) for dusting

½ cup (60 g) almond flour

1 cup (192 g) allulose sweetener

⅛ tsp sea salt

2 (¼-oz [7-g]) packets unflavored gelatin powder

6 tbsp (90 g) unsalted butter, melted

2 tsp (10 ml) vanilla extract

½ cup (120 ml) heavy whipping cream

1 egg

¼ cup (40 g) sugar-free milk chocolate chips (I prefer ChocZero or Lily's brand)

Nonstick cooking spray

MACROS PER SERVING

Calories: 209 | Protein: 7.3 g

Fat: 18.8 g | Net Carbs: 3.3 g

Fiber: 5.9 g | Sugar Alcohol: 21 g

Total Carbs: 30.2 g

Makes 9 brownies

Ooey Gooey Double Chocolate Brownies

I have so many wonderful memories of making brownies with my mom. And not much makes me happier than a warm brownie. These fudgy ones will be the best low-carb version you've ever had. They are actually chewy, like carb-filled brownies, and have a rich, fudgy center. I'm still dreaming of these brownies, even as I sit here typing this. Seriously, they are that good.

Try pairing this with the No-Churn Mint Chocolate Chip Ice Cream (page 130).

Arrange a rack in the center of your oven, and preheat it to 325°F (163°C).

In a mixing bowl, combine the cocoa powder, almond flour, allulose, sea salt, and gelatin. Use a whisk to fully mix the dry ingredients, ensuring no lumps remain. Then, add the butter, vanilla, cream, and egg, and mix well. Fold in the chocolate chips.

Generously grease a 9 x 9–inch (23 x 23–cm) baking pan with the cooking spray. Spread the batter evenly in the pan, and bake the brownies on the center rack for 20 to 25 minutes. The brownies are done when the edges are set and the center is just slightly jiggly and glossy.

Let the brownies cool on the countertop. Using a mesh sieve, evenly dust the top of the brownies with the cocoa powder, then cut them into nine pieces. Store wrapped leftovers in the fridge. If you serve the brownies a day or two after baking them, I suggest microwaving each brownie for 15 seconds to soften it before serving.

CRUMB CRUST

½ cup (60 g) almond flour

1 tbsp (5 g) coconut flour

2 tbsp (24 g) allulose sweetener

2 tsp (5 g) cinnamon

⅛ tsp sea salt

2 tbsp (30 g) unsalted butter, melted

CHEESECAKE BATTER

16 oz (455 g) cream cheese, softened

¼ cup (60 g) sour cream

2 eggs

1 cup + 2 tbsp (216 g) allulose sweetener, divided

1 tsp vanilla extract

¼ tsp sea salt

2 tbsp (30 g) unsalted butter, melted

1 tbsp (8 g) cinnamon

MACROS PER SERVING

Calories: 225 | Protein: 5 g
Fat: 20.1 g | Net Carbs: 2.8 g
Fiber: 1.7 g | Sugar Alcohol: 19 g
Total Carbs: 23.5 g

Makes 12 mini cheesecakes

Cinnamon Roll Cheesecake Bites

I have two favorite desserts: cinnamon rolls and cheesecake. So, I combined them—and Ketofied them—into perfect little bites! They are not too sweet and have just the right amount of gooey cinnamon in the middle. I quickly fell in love with this tasty mashup, and I hope you do too.

Start by preheating your oven to 275°F (135°C). Line a mini-cupcake tin with twelve paper liners.

To make the crust, mix together the almond flour, coconut flour, sweetener, cinnamon, salt, and butter. Fill each cupcake well with about 1 tablespoon (14 g) of crumb mixture, until the mixture is evenly divided in the wells, then use your fingers or a spoon to press the crumbs tightly and evenly at the bottom of each well.

For the batter, make sure your cream cheese is fully softened to room temperature before proceeding (see Pro Tip below). Use a stand mixer or electric hand mixer on low speed to beat the cream cheese until it's fluffy, then mix in the sour cream. Once they are combined, beat in 1 egg at a time, until the mixture is fully smooth. Add in 1 cup (192 g) of the allulose, the vanilla, and salt, and beat the mixture for 60 seconds. Divide the batter between the twelve cupcake wells.

To make the cinnamon swirl, combine the butter, cinnamon, and remaining 2 tablespoons (24 g) of allulose. Mix well, then spoon a circle of the cinnamon mixture on top of each of the twelve cakes. Use a toothpick or skewer to swirl the cinnamon mixture into the cakes. Bake the cakes for 20 to 25 minutes, or just until the top is glossy. Note: The centers will still be jiggly; they will gently finish cooking as they rest.

Let the cakes cool completely, then refrigerate them for 1 hour before serving. You can also make these ahead and store them in the fridge for up to 5 days.

Pro Tip: Forgot to leave out your cream cheese ahead of time? No problem! Place the cream cheese in a microwave-safe bowl and microwave it on 50 percent power in 20-second increments, until it's completely soft.

LEMON POUND CAKE

4 oz (113 g) cream cheese, softened

1½ cups (288 g) granulated sweetener

5 tbsp (75 g) unsalted butter, softened

5 eggs

1 tbsp (15 ml) vanilla extract

1½ cups (180 g) almond flour

2 tbsp (10 g) coconut flour

1 tsp baking powder

⅛ tsp sea salt

Zest of 1 lemon, finely grated

2 tbsp (30 ml) freshly squeezed lemon juice

LEMON CREAM CHEESE GLAZE

2 tbsp (32 g) cream cheese, softened

¼ cup (36 g) powdered sweetener (see Pro Tip)

1½ tbsp (23 ml) freshly squeezed lemon juice

Finely grated lemon zest

MACROS PER SERVING

Calories: 255 | Protein: 7.6 g
Fat: 22.5 g | Net Carbs: 3.1 g
Fiber: 2.3 g | Sugar Alcohol: 32 g
Total Carbs: 37.4 g

Serves 10 people

Lemon Pound Cake with Lemony Cream Cheese Glaze

Tart, bright, and perfect for breakfast or dessert, you'll never know this pound cake is Keto. Serve this at your next dinner party or Sunday brunch.

Preheat your oven to 300°F (149°C). Line the bottom of a loaf pan with parchment paper cut to size or grease the pan with cooking spray.

To make the cake, make sure your cream cheese is fully softened to room temperature (see the Pro Tip on page 125). Add it to the bowl of a stand mixer fitted with the paddle attachment. Beat it on low speed until it's fluffy, about 1 minute. Add the sweetener, and continue beating until the cream cheese and sweetener fully combine. Then, add in the butter. Beat the mixture for 1 minute, until it's uniform and fluffy. While the mixer is running on low speed, add the eggs, one at a time. Add the vanilla, almond flour, coconut flour, baking powder, and salt, and let the mixer run for 3 minutes, or until the batter is very well mixed. Add in the lemon zest and juice, and beat the mixture on high speed for 1 minute.

Pour the batter into the lined loaf pan, and bake the cake for 65 to 75 minutes, or until a toothpick inserted into the center comes out clean. Let the cake cool completely before removing it from the pan.

To make the glaze, be sure the cream cheese is fully softened. In a small mixing bowl, use a spatula to beat the cream cheese until it's smooth and slightly fluffy. Add the sweetener, and gently stir it into the cream cheese. This may seem dry, but continue stirring and the mixture will come together smoothly. Add the lemon juice, and stir until it's just combined.

When the cake is fully cooled, place it on a nice plate or platter. Then, drizzle the lemon glaze over the top. Use a spoon to spread the glaze evenly all over the top of the cake, letting some glaze drip over the edges. Refrigerate the cake for at least 30 minutes, or until the glaze sets. Garnish the cake with the lemon zest. Cut the cake into ten slices and serve!

Pro Tip: I prefer allulose as the sweetener in this recipe, but powdered allulose is very hard to find. You can make your own powdered sweetener by adding any granulated sweetener to a blender or food processor and letting it run on high speed for 5 minutes.

CHOCOLATE FUDGE SAUCE

¾ cup (144 g) allulose sweetener

⅓ cup (80 ml) heavy whipping cream

3 tbsp (45 g) unsalted butter

¼ cup (25 g) unsweetened cocoa powder, sifted

1 tsp vanilla extract

PEANUT BUTTER MOUSSE

8 oz (230 g) cream cheese, softened

½ cup (96 g) granulated sweetener

½ cup (130 g) 100% peanut butter with no added sugar

¼ tsp sea salt

1 cup (240 ml) heavy whipping cream

½ cup (70 g) salted peanuts, chopped, divided

MACROS PER SERVING

Calories: 578 | Protein: 13 g

Fat: 54.5 g | Net Carbs: 8.4 g

Fiber: 3.9 g | Sugar Alcohol: 40 g

Total Carbs: 52.3 g

Pro Tips: For a lower-carb and lower-calorie version, simply leave out the chocolate fudge. The peanut butter mousse is quite fabulous on its own!

You can also make the fudge sauce as a standalone recipe. Store it in a jar in the fridge, and drizzle it on your favorite ice cream.

Serves 6 people

Velvety Peanut Butter Cup Mousse with Homemade Chocolate Sauce

Layers of peanut butter mousse, gooey chocolate, and peanuts make this one of my favorite recipes in this book. The homemade chocolate sauce is a recipe my mom taught me, and it's a real treasure in our family. In fact, you can make the fudge sauce as a stand-alone recipe and pour it over a bowl of ice cream. Or just eat it by the spoonful right out of the jar—I won't tell anyone.

To make the chocolate sauce, in a saucepan over medium heat, whisk together the allulose, cream, and butter until the butter is melted, then add the cocoa powder and vanilla, whisking continuously to prevent lumps. Continue heating the sauce just until it is steamy, but not boiling. Turn off the heat, and pour the sauce into a jar or bowl to cool in the fridge for at least 30 minutes. You can also make this ahead, and refrigerate it for up to 14 days.

To make the mousse, make sure your cream cheese is fully softened to room temperature before proceeding (see the Pro Tip on page 125). In the bowl of a stand mixer fitted with the paddle attachment, beat the cream cheese on low speed for 2 minutes, or until it's very fluffy. If you don't have a stand mixer, you can mix this by hand. Add in the sweetener, peanut butter, and salt.

In a separate bowl, whisk the cream until stiff peaks form. With the mixer on low speed, add one-third of the whipped cream to the peanut butter mixture. Once combined, add another third, and repeat, until all of the whipped cream is fully mixed into the peanut butter mousse. Scrape the sides and bottom of the mixing bowl and continue mixing to ensure the mixture is fully smooth and without lumps.

Using six small 6- to 8-ounce (180- to 240-ml) drinking glasses, martini glasses, or small Mason jars, distribute half of the mousse into the cups by spooning it into the bottom of the glasses. Feeling chef-y? You can also do this with a piping bag. Drizzle the mousse with the fudge sauce, and sprinkle in some of the peanuts. Repeat with a second layer of peanut butter mousse, sauce, and peanuts.

Chill the mousse in the fridge for at least 1 hour, so it can set. You can make these a day or two ahead and refrigerate them, wrapped in plastic wrap.

2 cups (480 ml) heavy whipping cream

½ cup (96 g) allulose sweetener

3 egg yolks

⅛ tsp xanthan gum

2 tsp (10 ml) vanilla extract (see Pro Tip)

2 tsp (10 ml) peppermint extract

4–6 drops green food coloring (optional)

⅓ cup (54 g) sugar-free dark chocolate chips (I prefer ChocZero or Lily's brand)

MACROS PER SERVING

Calories: 251 | Protein: 2.2 g
Fat: 25.7 g | Net Carbs: 2.5 g
Fiber: 2.6 g | Sugar Alcohol: 12 g
Total Carbs: 17.1 g

Serves 8 people

No-Churn Mint Chocolate Chip Ice Cream

Mint chocolate chip ice cream is just one of those inexplicably nostalgic flavors for me. It really brings me back to my childhood, especially the days of working at Cold Stone Creamery in high school. And, this recipe does not require an ice cream maker, so anyone can make it at home. Even without churning, this ice cream stays soft and scoopable in the freezer. If for some reason you don't love mint ice cream—don't worry, I'm not judging you—this no-churn base works great with any flavor, so you can absolutely turn this ice cream into your favorite flavor.

Try pairing this with the Ooey Gooey Double Chocolate Brownies (page 122).

In a pot, combine the cream, allulose, and egg yolks. Place the pot over medium heat, and whisk the mixture continuously as it heats up, but do not let it boil. Use an instant-read thermometer to check that the base has reached 200°F (93°C), then take it off the heat. While whisking aggressively, add the xanthan gum, and continue whisking to prevent lumps. Then, stir in the vanilla and peppermint extracts and the food coloring, if using.

Pour the batter into a wide container, so it cools down quicker. I use a large plastic storage container with a cover. Freeze the ice cream overnight. The next day, stir in the chocolate chips and smooth the ice cream in the container. Freeze the ice cream for 2 hours before eating it. It will last in the freezer, covered, for several weeks—if you don't eat it all before then.

Pro Tip: Replace the vanilla extract with the seeds scraped out of one whole vanilla bean for a truly decadent touch.

CRUMB TOPPING

4 tbsp (60 g) unsalted butter, melted

1 cup (120 g) almond flour

1 cup (120 g) walnuts or pecans

¼ cup (48 g) granulated sweetener

⅛ tsp sea salt

BERRY FILLING

¾ cup (144 g) allulose sweetener

6 tbsp (90 g) unsalted butter

2 cups (280 g) sliced fresh strawberries

2 cups (280 g) blueberries

2 cups (240 g) raspberries

½ tsp vanilla extract

⅛ tsp sea salt

2 (¼-oz [7-g]) packets unflavored gelatin powder

MACROS PER SERVING

Calories: 366 | Protein: 8.5 g

Fat: 32.6 g | Net Carbs: 9.9 g

Fiber: 6.5 g | Sugar Alcohol: 24 g

Total Carbs: 40.4 g

Serves 8 people

Triple Berry Crisp

A spoonful of this crisp will have you swooning. It's so easy to make, and the fresh fruit provides the perfect balance of tart and sweet. The crumb topping brings the perfect salty crunch to the party, and you can prepare this as four small tarts or in one pie pan. Either way, your dinner guests will be happy. Serve this with fresh whipped cream or a scoop of ice cream.

Preheat your oven to 425°F (218°C).

To make the crumb topping, pulse the butter, almond flour, walnuts, sweetener, and salt in a food processor, just until the ingredients are uniform and crumbly, like wet sand. Set the crumb topping aside.

For the berry filling, in a saucepan over medium heat, melt the allulose and butter completely, stirring occasionally. When the butter is melted, whisk the mixture together and simmer it for about 3 minutes, until it becomes a light brown color and is very foamy and bubbly. Add the strawberries, blueberries, raspberries, vanilla, and salt, and stir to combine. Let the berries cook for 3 minutes, then remove the pan from the heat.

Very gently stir in the gelatin, making sure the gelatin is dissolved with no lumps, but without breaking up the berries. Pour the fruit mixture into either four small ungreased tart pans or one pie tin.

Top the filling with the crumb topping, and bake the crisp for 10 minutes, or just until the crumb topping is golden brown and toasted.

To serve, I recommend letting the crisp cool down completely in the fridge for a few hours to allow the fruit filling to set. But you can absolutely eat it warm, just know the filling will be runnier.

Pro Tip: Save money by buying nuts like pecans, walnuts, and almonds in the baking aisle at the grocery store, rather than the snack aisle. The nuts for baking are significantly lower in price.

Nonstick cooking spray

6 eggs, 5 separated and 1 whole, divided

4 oz (113 g) cream cheese, softened

4 tbsp (60 g) unsalted butter, melted

¼ cup (61 g) unsweetened coconut cream

1 tbsp (15 ml) vanilla extract

2 tsp (10 ml) coconut extract

1½ cups (180 g) almond flour

¼ cup (25 g) coconut flour

1½ cups (180 g) granulated sweetener

1 tsp baking powder

¼ tsp salt

1 cup (120 g) unsweetened coconut flakes

COCONUT CREAM CHEESE FROSTING

16 oz (455 g) cream cheese, softened

16 tbsp (240 g) unsalted butter, softened

1½ cups (216 g) powdered sweetener (see Pro Tip on page 126)

1 tsp vanilla extract

½ tsp coconut extract

½ cup (60 g) unsweetened coconut flakes

MACROS PER SERVING

Calories: 444 | Protein: 8.1 g

Fat: 41.6 g | Net Carbs: 4.1 g

Fiber: 3.3 g | Sugar Alcohol: 32 g

Total Carbs: 39.4 g

Serves 16 people

Coconut Cake with Coconut Cream Cheese Frosting

My mom and I made this Ketofied version of coconut cake together on her last visit to Austin. She loves coconut, and so this cake is for her. The sponge cake is moist and just light enough, and the cream cheese frosting, infused with coconut, is so good you'll be fighting over who can lick the spatula. Thanks, Mom, for inspiring me every day.

Arrange a rack in the center of your oven and preheat it to 350°F (180°C). Grease two 8-inch (20-cm) round cake pans with cooking spray.

Using an electric hand mixer with a mixing bowl or stand mixer fitted with the whisk attachment, whip the 5 egg whites for 3 to 4 minutes, or until stiff peaks form, then set the egg whites aside. In a clean mixing bowl, add the softened cream cheese and whip on medium speed for 1 minute, or until the cream cheese is fluffy. Then add the melted butter and mix for another 30 seconds, or until fully combined. Stir in the coconut cream, vanilla, coconut extract, almond flour, coconut flour, sweetener, baking powder, salt, and coconut flakes. Then, add the egg yolks and remaining whole egg. Mix really well to combine the ingredients, then gently fold in the whipped egg whites a little at a time, until all the egg whites are just combined with the batter. Divide the batter equally into the two cake pans, then smooth the batter evenly.

Bake the cakes on the center rack for 20 minutes, or until a toothpick inserted into the center comes out clean. Remove the cakes from the oven, and refrigerate them to cool them completely before removing them from the pans.

To make the frosting, first make sure your cream cheese (see the Pro Tip on page 125) and butter are completely soft and at room temperature. In a stand mixer with the paddle attachment, mix the cream cheese and butter on low speed until the ingredients are combined and the mixture is fluffy, about 4 minutes. Then, add the sweetener, vanilla, and coconut extract, and continue mixing on low speed for at least 2 minutes, or until the frosting is fluffy and smooth.

To assemble, place one layer of the cake on a cake stand or large plate. Add a ½-inch (1.3-cm) layer of frosting on top, then place the second layer of cake on the frosting. Completely cover the cake with frosting, using a spatula or bench scraper to smooth it. Then coat the sides of the cake with the coconut flakes.

PECAN CRUST

1½ cups (180 g) unsalted pecans

2 tbsp (20 g) almond flour

1 egg white

¼ cup (48 g) granulated sweetener

¼ tsp sea salt

Nonstick cooking spray

STRAWBERRY CLOUD MOUSSE

1 lb (455 g) strawberries, sliced

2 egg whites

1 cup (192 g) allulose sweetener

1 tsp vanilla extract

1 tbsp (15 ml) freshly squeezed lemon juice

FOR SERVING

Chopped strawberries or whipped cream (optional)

MACROS PER SERVING

Calories: 193 | Protein: 4.2 g

Fat: 17.3 g | Net Carbs: 4.6 g

Fiber: 3.5 g | Sugar Alcohol: 24 g

Total Carbs: 32.1 g

Serves 8 people

Magical Strawberry Icebox Pie

This recipe is something my mom would make every year for Passover. I call it magical for two reasons. One, it's truly too good to believe. Two, when you're making it, the steps don't really make any sense. In fact, the last time I saw my mom make this, she put the egg whites and strawberries in the stand mixer, and I said, "Mom, this isn't going to work." She said, "Mike, trust me. . . . It's magic." Needless to say, it worked, of course. And thus, the pie got its name: Magical Strawberry Icebox Pie.

To make the crust, preheat your oven to 325°F (163°C). In a food processor, pulse the pecans, almond flour, egg white, sweetener, and salt, just until a uniform crumble forms.

Grease the bottom and sides of a 9-inch (23-cm) pie pan with the nonstick cooking spray, then press the crust mixture evenly into the bottom of the pan. You can use a sheet of parchment on top to help you press out the mixture evenly. Bake the crust for 12 to 15 minutes, or until it's toasted and golden brown. Set the pan aside to cool the crust completely.

To make the magical mousse, place the sliced strawberries, egg whites, allulose, vanilla, and lemon juice in the bowl of a stand mixer fitted with the whisk attachment. Starting on slow speed, and then gradually increasing the speed over the time, beat the mixture for 10 to 12 minutes. The mixture will whip up, inflate, and almost fill the entire mixing bowl. You'll know it's done when the mousse holds stiff peaks—it will stand straight up when you lift the whisk—and has a nice pink color.

Pour the mixture onto the cooled crust, smooth the top with a spatula, and place the pie directly into the freezer. Note: Depending on how much your eggs fluff up, you may have extra mousse that didn't fit in the pan. Fortunately, this is a wonderful bonus—chef's kiss! Pour it into little cups, and freeze it for later as personal strawberry mousse cups.

To serve, bring the pie out of the freezer just before serving—it will melt if it's out of the freezer for too long. And, don't worry, it stays soft and fluffy in the freezer; it's just another unique property of this magical cake. Cut the pie into eight slices, and serve it with the strawberries on top and whipped cream, if using.

THE (NOT-SO-BASIC) basics

Looking for a few yummy Keto-friendly staples and sauces? Well, you bread my mind! Craft your own creative meals with these bonus recipes to help you stay on track. I mean, who doesn't love some good, crusty garlic bread with dinner (page 143)? Or, a perfect homemade pancake recipe for those Sunday mornings at home (page 147)? Let's toast to these simple staples you can keep in your back pocket for any meal.

Low-Carb Cheddar Bay Biscuits	140
Cheesy Garlic Breadsticks	143
Keto Cornbread	144
Fluffy Waffles & Pancakes	147
Crispy Rosemary Sea Salt Crackers	148

½ cup (15 g) grated Parmesan cheese

1 cup (120 g) almond flour

1 tbsp (12 g) granulated sweetener

1 tbsp (15 g) baking powder

2 tsp (5 g) onion powder

¼ tsp sea salt

2 tbsp (30 g) cold salted butter

½ cup + 2 tbsp (50 g) shredded cheddar cheese, divided

1 egg

⅛ tsp dried parsley

MACROS PER SERVING

Calories: 228 | Protein: 10.6 g
Fat: 19.4 g | Net Carbs: 4 g
Fiber: 2.2 g | Sugar Alcohol: 2 g
Total Carbs: 8.2 g

Makes 6 biscuits

Low-Carb Cheddar Bay Biscuits

Am I the only one that went to Red Lobster just for the warm biscuits? Well, now you don't have to give them up on a Keto or gluten-free diet. You can make them yourself, and without all the carbs! Flaky, salty, and cheesy, these are a real treat. If you're feeding a crowd, I'd suggest doubling this recipe.

Try pairing these with the Giant Showstopping Meatballs in Rosé Sauce (page 45).

Preheat your oven to 350°F (180°C). Line a cookie sheet with parchment paper and set it aside.

In a large mixing bowl, mix the Parmesan, almond flour, sweetener, baking powder, onion powder, and salt until the ingredients are combined. Then, cut the cold butter into small cubes and add them to the bowl. Use a wooden spoon or your fingers to press the butter into the dry ingredients. Continue kneading the mixture together for a minute or two, until it is well combined, with no large lumps of butter remaining. Add ½ cup (40 g) of the cheddar and the egg, and mix again until the ingredients are well combined.

Form the dough into one smooth ball, then divide it into six even balls of dough. Press the six balls slightly flat onto the lined baking sheet. (You can also make this in a muffin tin by simply dividing the dough into six wells of a greased muffin tin.) Then, sprinkle some of the remaining 2 tablespoons (10 g) of cheddar on top of each biscuit, and sprinkle the biscuits with the parsley.

Bake the biscuits for 15 to 20 minutes, or just until they are lightly golden brown. Let the biscuits cool before removing them from the tray. You can serve them warm or at room temperature. Either way, they won't last long on your table.

2¼ cups (180 g) shredded mozzarella cheese, divided

2 oz (57 g) cream cheese

½ cup (60 g) almond flour

¾ cup (22 g) grated Parmesan cheese, divided

2 tbsp (18 g) garlic powder

½ tsp sea salt

1 egg

3 tbsp (45 g) salted butter, softened

6 cloves garlic, minced

½ tsp Italian herb blend

MACROS PER SERVING

Calories: 203 | Protein: 8.2 g
Fat: 17.2 g | Net Carbs: 4.8 g
Fiber: 1.4 g | Total Carbs: 6.2 g

Serves 6 people

Cheesy Garlic Breadsticks

Are we allowed to eat just garlic bread as a meal? If so, sign me up. Crispy, chewy, and oozing with garlic butter, this goes great on the side of nearly any dinner—or as the main course! These really remind me of pizza delivery breadsticks and are certainly going to bring smiles to the whole family. You can also have fun with this recipe and use this as the base for a flatbread. Try topping it with sliced tomatoes and rosemary, or mozzarella and cremini mushrooms, for a fun appetizer or meal.

Try pairing this with the Giant Showstopping Meatballs in Rosé Sauce (page 45).

Arrange a rack in the center of your oven, and preheat it to 400°F (204°C). Line a baking sheet with parchment paper.

Place 2 cups (160 g) of the mozzarella and the cream cheese in a microwave-safe mixing bowl. Microwave the cheeses on high for 60 seconds, and stir them well to combine. Microwave in 30-second increments as needed, until the cheeses are fully melted and smooth.

Add the almond flour, ½ cup (15 g) of the Parmesan, garlic powder, salt, and the egg, and mix the ingredients aggressively. Keep mixing until the mixture becomes a uniform dough. Scoop the dough onto the lined baking sheet, and use a spatula to spread the dough into an oval shape that's about ½ inch (1.3 cm) thick.

Add the butter, garlic, and Italian herbs to the mixing bowl. Stir well to make the garlic compound butter. Spread the butter evenly on the top of the dough. Then, top it with the remaining ¼ cup (20 g) of mozzarella and the remaining ¼ cup (7 g) of Parmesan.

Bake the bread for about 30 minutes on the center rack, or until it's dark brown and crispy on top. Let it cool slightly before cutting it into six strips.

Nonstick cooking spray

1 (15-oz [425-g]) can baby corn, drained

1 tsp sea salt

2 cups (240 g) almond flour

2 tbsp (24 g) granulated sweetener

½ tsp turmeric, for color

2 eggs

MACROS PER SERVING

Calories: 132 | Protein: 5.6 g
Fat: 10.6 g | Net Carbs: 2.6 g
Fiber: 3 g | Sugar Alcohol: 2 g
Total Carbs: 7.6 g

Makes 12 servings

Keto Cornbread

Keto cornbread? Is it really possible? Well, this recipe uses baby corn as the base, since baby corn is significantly lower in carbs than sweet corn! Now, I know cornbread can be a controversial topic. Sweet versus savory is a hot-button political issue in the U.S. But my feeling is that I never met a cornbread I didn't like, so this bipartisan version meets somewhere in the middle. This recipe is slightly sweet, but if you like a sweeter cornbread, double the sweetener, since this is more of a Southern-style savory cornbread.

Try pairing this with the Low & Slow Texas Brisket Chili (page 50).

Preheat your oven to 350°F (180°C). Then grease a 9 x 9–inch (23 x 23–cm) baking dish with the cooking spray.

Pulse the corn in a food processor several times, just until rice-sized pieces form. Place a clean dish towel or piece of cheesecloth on your counter, and scrape out the corn from the processor right onto the towel. Wring out the corn to squeeze out as much water as you can from it. Then, place the dry corn in a large mixing bowl.

Add the salt, almond flour, sweetener, turmeric, and eggs, and mix well to create the batter. Spread the batter into your greased baking dish, and smooth out the top surface. Bake the cornbread for 30 minutes, or until the top is lightly browned and set. Let the cornbread cool completely before cutting it into 12 pieces.

Pro Tip: Add thinly sliced jalapeño and/or shredded cheddar to the top of the cornbread before baking it for a delicious jalapeño-cheddar cornbread.

WAFFLES OR PANCAKES

3 eggs

¼ cup (48 g) granulated sweetener

1 tbsp (15 ml) heavy whipping cream

¾ cup (90 g) almond flour

⅛ tsp xanthan gum

Nonstick cooking spray

FOR SERVING

Pats of butter and sugar-free syrup

MACROS PER SERVING

Calories: 375 | Protein: 18 g
Fat: 31.6 g | Net Carbs: 5.5 g
Fiber: 4.8 g | Sugar Alcohol: 24 g
Total Carbs: 34.3 g

Serves 2 people (2 large waffles or 4 pancakes)

Fluffy Waffles & Pancakes

Let's be honest, waffles and pancakes covered in sugary syrup are not exactly the healthiest breakfast option. But they're just too dang good! Well, now you have a better choice. This waffle and pancake batter is totally guilt-free, and perfect for kids and adults alike. Make this for breakfast, brunch, or dessert, and lose none of the yumminess of a big stack of pancakes or waffles. This is just as good—or better!

In a mixing bowl, aggressively whisk together the eggs, sweetener, cream, almond flour, and xanthan gum until there are no lumps. You can do this by hand, or use an electric mixer. Let the batter sit for 2 minutes to rest.

For waffles, warm up your electric waffle iron. Spray it with cooking spray, and pour half the batter into the waffle iron. Cook for the time specified for your waffle iron, or until golden brown. Repeat with the remaining batter. For a crispier waffle, place a finished waffle directly on the oven rack in a 350°F (180°C) oven, and bake it for 5 minutes.

For pancakes, warm up a skillet or griddle over medium-low heat. Spray it with cooking spray, and pour the batter, making four pancakes, onto the griddle. Cook the pancakes for 2 minutes, or until the batter gets bubbly, then flip them and repeat for the other side.

For serving, top the waffles or pancakes with a pat of the butter, and drizzle them with the sugar-free syrup.

Pro Tip: Make the Pickle-Brined Crispy Chicken Tendies with Homemade Ranch (page 16) and combine it with these waffles for an amazing take on chicken and waffles!

1 cup (30 g) grated Parmesan cheese

½ cup (60 g) almond flour

2 tbsp (10 g) coconut flour

2 egg whites

⅛ tsp + ¼ tsp sea salt, divided

¼ tsp cumin

2 tsp (1 g) fresh rosemary, very finely minced

MACROS PER SERVING

Calories: 120 | Protein: 7.5 g

Fat: 9.2 g | Net Carbs: 2.2 g

Fiber: 1.8 g | Total Carbs: 4 g

Pro Tip: Use a rolling pin with adjustable rings for thickness to get the crackers perfectly thin and even. These rolling pins use removable rings to control exactly how thick your dough will roll out. One would be a fantastic addition to your kitchen if you bake a lot, and cost about $15 on popular shopping websites. Just search for "adjustable rolling pin" in the search bar.

Serves 4 people

Crispy Rosemary Sea Salt Crackers

What's better than a salty snack? I had to ditch the Cheez-Its and Ritz Crackers, but these are the perfect replacement! They go great with a good dip; you can find a few in the next chapter (page 151). Or, top the crackers with deli meat and cheese for a protein-packed snack.

Try pairing this with the Greek Roasted Garlic & Feta Dip (page 160).

Arrange a rack in the center of your oven, and preheat it to 350°F (180°C). Cut two 15 x 20–inch (38 x 50–cm) pieces of parchment paper, and set them on your counter.

In a large mixing bowl, mix the Parmesan, almond flour, coconut flour, egg whites, ⅛ teaspoon of the salt, cumin, and rosemary until the ingredients are very well combined. Use your hands to knead the dough for 1 to 2 minutes. It will feel a bit dry and crumbly, but keep working it until it's smooth. Roll the dough into a ball, and place it onto one of the pieces of parchment paper. Loosely place the other sheet of parchment on top of the dough ball, and let the dough rest for 15 minutes.

With the second piece of parchment on top, use your hands to start pressing and smoothing out the dough between the parchment papers into a rough rectangular shape as thin as you can get it.

Then, use a rolling pin to very evenly spread the dough into a thin sheet. Take your time with this, and work the dough from the center outward, spreading it out as thin as you can (aim for ⅛ inch [4 mm]); see the Pro Tip. You'll notice the edges will start to splay and crack—that's OK! Once you get the dough very thin, cut off the cracked edges, and press them back into the dough. Use the rolling pin to smooth it all out, repeating the steps as needed, until you have a thin, rectangular-shaped dough. Slide the parchment paper with the dough onto a baking sheet. Remove the top layer of parchment, sprinkle the dough with the remaining ¼ teaspoon of salt, and use a pizza cutter to cut the dough into 1-inch (3-cm) squares in a grid pattern.

Bake the dough for 25 to 30 minutes on the center rack of the oven, or until the crackers are evenly brown. Check the crackers often toward the end of the cooking time so they don't burn.

Let the crackers cool completely, and then break them apart at the seams. The crackers may be stored, in an airtight container, for up to 5 days at room temperature or 2 weeks in the fridge.

WHEN
I DIP,
YOU DIP,
we dip

Perfect for a party or for next-level snacking, these are nacho ordinary dips. Spicy, cheesy, and with all the flavors of home, these are packed with fun! Not to mention, they have a few Keto surprises along the way, to ensure they fit your low-carb lifestyle. And, in queso didn't know, these dips go fantastic with the homemade cracker recipe (page 148).

Buffalo Chicken Pimento Dip	152
Restaurant-Style White Queso	155
Everything-but-the-Bagel Dip	156
Spicy Maryland Crab Dip	159
Greek Roasted Garlic & Feta Dip	160

BUFFALO CHICKEN DIP

4 oz (113 g) cream cheese, softened

¼ cup (60 g) mayonnaise

1 tsp garlic powder

¼ tsp black pepper

2 tbsp (30 ml) Frank's Red Hot sauce

1 (4-oz [120-ml]) jar diced pimento peppers, drained

1 cup (80 g) shredded cheddar cheese

1 cup (149 g) cooked shredded chicken (I use leftover rotisserie chicken)

FOR SERVING

Shredded cheddar cheese or bleu cheese crumbles, celery and carrot sticks, and bell pepper slices (optional)

MACROS PER SERVING

Calories: 225 | Protein: 12.1 g

Fat: 18.4 g | Net Carbs: 1.5 g

Fiber: 0.2 g | Total Carbs: 1.7 g

Serves 6 people

Buffalo Chicken Pimento Dip

This tasty mash-up is good hot or cold. Spicy, cheesy, and packed with protein, I can eat this dip right out of the bowl. It's perfect for your next party or game day. The pimento peppers add a wonderful bite of sweet and tangy flavor and make for the yummiest dip. For the chicken, I like using rotisserie chicken from the grocery store, but you can also use canned chicken or any leftover cooked chicken you have on hand.

In a mixing bowl, beat the cream cheese and the mayo until it's combined and fluffy. Then, add in the garlic powder, pepper, and hot sauce. Mix until the ingredients are well combined, then gently stir in the pimentos, cheddar, and chicken. Stir just until combined, but not overmixed. I like some larger pieces of chicken to remain in the dip for texture.

I prefer to serve this as is, but it's also good warm. Top it with the cheese, and serve it with the celery and carrot sticks and bell peppers, if using. To warm it up, place it in an oven-safe dish, and bake it at 400°F (204°C) for 15 minutes, then top it with the cheese.

Pro Tip: This can be turned into a bonus dinner recipe—buffalo chicken–stuffed peppers! Use this recipe as the filling for three halved and seeded red bell peppers. Top the peppers with shredded cheddar and bake them at 400°F (204°C) for 20 minutes, or until the stuffing is bubbly. Et voila! Dinner is served.

QUESTO

½ lb (230 g) white American cheese, from the deli counter

10 oz (280 g) Oaxaca cheese or freshly shredded mozzarella cheese

1 cup (240 ml) heavy whipping cream

1 (7-oz [198-g]) can mild or hot green chiles, drained

¼ tsp crushed red pepper

½ tsp sea salt

FOR SERVING

Fresh cilantro, jalapeño slices, and/or pico de gallo (optional)

Pork rinds or sliced vegetables (optional)

MACROS PER SERVING

Calories: 263 | Protein: 16.5 g

Fat: 21 g | Net Carbs: 3.6 g

Fiber: 0.8 g | Total Carbs: 4.4 g

Serves 8 people

Restaurant-Style White Queso

Give me a big bowl of chips and queso, and I'm a happy camper. This recipe is so easy you'll wonder why you never made this before. For a bonus dinner idea, sear and slice a steak or even boneless chicken, and pour this queso over the top. Yum! Note: For this recipe, do not use packaged shredded cheese, as it contains a starch coating that could hurt the texture of the finished queso.

Start by breaking up the American cheese into small pieces. Then shred the Oaxaca cheese.

To a saucepan, add the cream and the two cheeses, and stir to combine the ingredients. Place the pan on your stove over medium-low heat. Let the cheese and cream mixture gently melt, stirring regularly. Once the mixture starts to steam and get hot, start stirring more aggressively. Eventually, all the cheese will be fully melted. Stir once more until the mixture is uniformly melted. This will take about 6 minutes, but make sure it never comes to a full boil, as that could "break" the cheese sauce. Adjust the heat as needed.

Then, add the green chiles, red pepper, and salt. Let the mixture simmer for 2 minutes.

For serving, pour the queso into a dipping bowl, garnish it with the cilantro, jalapeño, and pico de gallo, if using. Serve the pork rinds or vegetables on the side, if using.

Pro Tip: Take this recipe up a notch by adding sautéed chorizo. Find a tube of fresh pork chorizo in the refrigerator section of your grocery store, near the breakfast sausage. Sauté it in a pan until it's browned, about 6 to 8 minutes, and place it on top of the finished queso.

SALMON DIP

1 (6-oz [170-g]) can skinless and boneless salmon, drained

3 oz (85 g) Nova Lox or smoked salmon (see Pro Tips)

8 oz (230 g) cream cheese, softened

2 tbsp (19 g) Everything seasoning (I prefer Trader Joe's brand)

1 tbsp (12 g) capers

1 tbsp (15 ml) caper juice from the jar

½ red onion, sliced

FOR SERVING

1 tsp Everything seasoning

1 tbsp (12 g) capers

¼ red onion, diced

1 cucumber, sliced, or Crispy Rosemary Sea Salt Crackers (page 148)

MACROS PER SERVING

Calories: 208 | Protein: 13.4 g

Fat: 15.2 g | Net Carbs: 3.5 g

Fiber: 0.6 g | Total Carbs: 4.1 g

Serves 6 people

Everything-but-the-Bagel Dip

Growing up on the East Coast, trips to New York City were something I always looked forward to. Driving up I-95, I knew a good bagel with a schmear wasn't far away. So, this recipe brings back all the feelings of a good lox bagel, but without the carbs. This recipe is dedicated to Debbie Roth, who was like a second mother to me, and our dear family friend. She was a wonderful cook, and made a salmon dip for brunches and holiday parties. This recipe will always make me think of her. I miss you, Debbie.

In a food processor, pulse the salmon, lox, cream cheese, Everything seasoning, capers, caper juice, and onion repeatedly, until the ingredients combine, less than a minute. Then run the processor on low speed, until the mixture is smooth and fluffy. Spoon the dip into a serving bowl, and smooth out the top.

To serve, sprinkle the top with the Everything seasoning, capers, and onion. Use the cucumbers for dipping.

Pro Tips: Don't like smoked salmon? Just leave out the lox, and it's still a delicious salmon dip!

Use this dip as a sandwich filling for a fantastic lunch or snack on the go!

OLD BAY DIP

16 oz (455 g) cream cheese

½ cup (120 g) mayonnaise

Zest of 1 lemon, finely grated

½ tbsp (8 g) Dijon mustard

1 tbsp (7 g) onion powder

1 tbsp (9 g) garlic powder

1 tbsp (3 g) dried dill

1½ tbsp (11 g) Old Bay Seasoning

1½ cups (120 g) shredded cheddar cheese, divided

3 scallions, sliced and separated into white and green

1 lb (455 g) lump crabmeat

FOR SERVING

Pork rinds, sliced vegetables, or Crispy Rosemary Sea Salt Crackers (page 148) (optional)

MACROS PER SERVING

Calories: 382 | Protein: 13.1 g

Fat: 35.1 g | Net Carbs: 4.1 g

Fiber: 0.4 g | Total Carbs: 4.5 g

Serves 8 people

Spicy Maryland Crab Dip

Growing up in Maryland, I was lucky enough to have the freshest blue crabs. In fact, I'd often go crabbing with my dad in the summertime. This crab dip will bring you right back to the beach. Just make sure you splurge on high-quality, USA lump crabmeat when you can find it. It's really worth it here, as the farmed crabmeat from abroad is just not as good.

Preheat your oven to 400°F (204°C).

In a mixing bowl, microwave the cream cheese on high for 60 seconds, or until it's warm and very soft. Use a spatula or spoon to whip the cream cheese just until it's fluffy, then add in the mayo, lemon zest, Dijon, onion powder, garlic powder, dill, Old Bay, and 1 cup (80 g) of the cheddar cheese. Stir well to combine the ingredients, then stir in just the white half of the scallions. Gently fold in the crabmeat just until mixed; do not overmix.

Pour the crab dip into a small cast-iron or broiler-safe dish. Spread the dip into an even layer, and top it with the remaining ½ cup (40 g) of cheddar.

Bake the dip in the oven for 15 minutes, then switch the oven to broil and broil the dip for 2 to 3 minutes, or until the top browns. Keep an eye on the dip, so it doesn't burn.

To serve, sprinkle the green scallion slices on the dip, and serve it with the pork rinds, vegetables, or crackers, if using.

Pro Tip: Bonus recipe! Turn this into crab-stuffed salmon by cutting a slit into four 8-ounce (227-g) salmon fillets and using this recipe as the filling. Stuff the salmon with the crab dip, then place the fillets on a baking sheet, sprinkle with ½ teaspoon of sea salt, and bake for 25 minutes at 400°F (204°C). Yum!

GREEK DIP

½ yellow onion, diced

½ cup (50 g) whole cloves garlic

¼ cup (36 g) Kalamata olives, halved

¼ tsp black pepper

2 tsp (2 g) dried oregano

Zest of 1 lemon, grated

¼ cup (60 ml) extra virgin olive oil

14–16 oz (400–455 g) feta cheese, a block or in brine

½ cup (120 ml) plain Greek yogurt or sour cream

FOR SERVING

Fresh parsley leaves

Sliced vegetables or Crispy Rosemary Sea Salt Crackers (page 148)

MACROS PER SERVING

Calories: 231 | Protein: 8.1 g
Fat: 20.1 g | Net Carbs: 5.2 g
Fiber: 0.4 g | Total Carbs: 5.6 g

Serves 8 people

Greek Roasted Garlic & Feta Dip

This tasty dip works great for a party, or even as a bold addition to your next charcuterie board. Salty, garlicky, and packed with healthy fats, this dip is so yummy your guests will be very impressed. Did I mention it was garlicky, because all that garlic slowly roasts in the olive oil, and becomes buttery, sweet, and caramelized. Yum! You'll just have to try it for yourself. Don't like feta? This also works great with brie or cream cheese.

Preheat your oven to 325°F (163°C). In a 9 x 9–inch (23 x 23–cm) square or round baking dish, add the onion, garlic, olives, pepper, oregano, lemon zest, and olive oil. Stir everything in the pan to combine the ingredients. Then, make a spot for the feta in the middle, by pushing most of the ingredients to the edges. Nestle the feta right into the center, and place the dish in the oven, uncovered, for 1 hour.

Remove the dip from the oven, and carefully use the back of a spoon to smash the cloves of garlic right in the pan. Stir everything well to combine, as the feta will be warm and soft. Then, stir in the yogurt or sour cream until it's fully combined.

Top the dip with the parsley leaves, and serve it right out of the baking dish with the vegetables or crackers.

Pro Tip: Turn this dip into a fantastic roasted garlic & feta-stuffed chicken for dinner! Take 2 pounds (910 g) of boneless chicken breasts, cut a slit in the middle, and stuff them with the feta dip. Top them with ½ teaspoon of sea salt and shredded mozzarella or Parmesan. Bake the breasts at 375°F (190°C) for 30 to 35 minutes, or until the center of the chicken reads 165°F (74°C) on an instant-read thermometer. Opa!

ABOUT THE AUTHOR

As an author, private chef, and TV personality, Michael Silverstein is passionate about the power of cooking to improve one's life. After beating out tens of thousands of competitors on Season 10 of *MasterChef* on FOX, Chef Michael has secured his spot as one of the best cooks in America. He is enthusiastic about teaching others how to cook healthy, delicious meals, and he firmly believes that anyone can make incredible food at home. After losing more than 80 pounds (36 kg) in 1 year on the Ketogenic diet, Michael hopes to continue sharing his message that healthy food is beautiful and can be enjoyed by all eaters, Keto or not.

Michael is the bestselling author of *New Keto Cooking*, and has been featured in *People* magazine, Hallmark Channel, NPR, *New York Post*, *National Examiner*, *Closer Weekly*, Delish, Medium, Diply, feedfeed, *Out Front* magazine, *Pittsburgh Post-Gazette*, Great Day Houston, CBS San Diego, *Good Day Atlanta*, and more.

Most of the time, you can find Michael cooking at home with his fiancé, Jacob, and their rescue dog and cat. But when he's not in the kitchen, he enjoys biking, gardening, playing piano, traveling, and exploring the Austin food scene.

For more of his recipes, find Michael on Instagram @chefmichael.keto, or on his website www.chef-michael.com. You can also listen to Michael's podcast, *The Talk with Chef Michael*, on Spotify, iTunes, or YouTube. And, make sure to pick up a copy of his first book, *New Keto Cooking*, at any major retailer.

ACKNOWLEDGMENTS

You, yes you! I deeply thank you for being here and for letting me share my food and my heart with you. Happy cooking!

Thank you to my parents, Roni and Bob, for believing in me and for sharing your never-ending wisdom and love. Thank you to my sisters, Jaimee and Laura, for the long phone calls and many laughs. Big shoutout to my awesome nieces and nephews, Eitan, Yael, Iris, Kyla, and Henry. I love you!

Thank you to my dear friends, who continue to put up with me, for some reason. Cheers!

Thank you to the Keto community! You inspire me to keep going, and I certainly wouldn't be here without your support and friendship. #ketofam

A huge thanks to Caitlin, Will, Meg, and the entire Page Street Publishing team, for giving me another chance to follow my dreams.

And, thank you, Jacob, my heart and soul. I am who I am because of you. I love you.

INDEX

5-Hour Short Rib Beef Stew, 95

A
allulose sweetener, 10
    Chinese Restaurant Sesame Chicken, 23
    Cinnamon Roll Cheesecake Bites, 125
    No-Churn Mint Chocolate Chip Ice Cream, 130
    Ooey Gooey Double Chocolate Brownies, 122
    Slow Cooker BBQ Pulled Pork, 65
    Sticky "Hot Honey" Chicken Wings, 20
    Sugarless Shrimp Pad Thai, 80
    Sweet Teriyaki-Glazed Salmon, 79
    Triple Berry Crisp, 133
    Velvety Peanut Butter Cup Mousse with Homemade Chocolate Sauce, 129
American cheese, 155. *See also* cheese
animal fat, 11
apple cider vinegar
    Filipino-Inspired Chicken Adobo, 28
    Pepper-Crusted Tuna Steak with Sesame Ginger Chimichurri, 84
    Slow Cooker BBQ Pulled Pork, 65
    Sticky "Hot Honey" Chicken Wings, 20
    Sweet Teriyaki-Glazed Salmon, 79
avocado oil, 11
    Blackened Salmon in Creamy Cajun Sauce, 83
    Brisket for the Holidays, 54
    Cauliflower Dirty Rice, 116
    Chinese Restaurant Sesame Chicken, 23
    Classic Italian Chicken Marsala, 27
    Crispy Garlic Butter Steak, 42
    Curried Butternut Squash Bisque, 100
    Garlic Parmesan Green Beans, 112
    Giant Showstopping Meatballs in Rosé Sauce, 45
    Grilled Carne Asada with Homemade Salsa Roja, 46
    Guilt-Free Creamy Pasta Florentine, 69
    Jalapeño Popper–Stuffed Burgers with "Animal Sauce," 38
    Little Fancy Steak au Poivre, A, 53
    Low & Slow Texas Brisket Chili, 50
    Pepper-Crusted Tuna Steak with Sesame Ginger Chimichurri, 84
    Philly Cheesesteak—Hold the Bun!, 49
    Sausage, Peppers, & Onions with Spicy Creole Aioli, 66
    Smoky Southwest Chicken Picante, 35
    Sugarless Shrimp Pad Thai, 80
    Sweet Teriyaki-Glazed Salmon, 79

B
bacon
    Best Damn Keto Pizza Ever!, The, 58
    Fall-Off-the-Bone Ribs with Mike's Coffee Dry Rub, 61

    Guilt-Free Creamy Pasta Florentine, 69
    Million-Dollar Lasagna Roll-Ups, 62
    Sausage, Peppers, & Onions with Spicy Creole Aioli, 66
    Slow Cooker BBQ Pulled Pork, 65
Bacon & Bleu Coleslaw, 119
balsamic vinegar
    5-Hour Short Rib Beef Stew, 95
    Low & Slow Texas Brisket Chili, 50
    Sheet Pan Pesto Chicken with Jammy Tomatoes, 32
basics food/meals
    Cheesy Garlic Breadsticks, 143
    Crispy Rosemary Sea Salt Crackers, 148
    Fluffy Waffles & Pancakes, 147
    Keto Cornbread, 144
    Low-Carb Cheddar Bay Biscuits, 140
basil
    Giant Showstopping Meatballs in Rosé Sauce, 45
    Guilt-Free Creamy Pasta Florentine, 69
    "Hangover" Beef Pho, 99
    Sheet Pan Pesto Chicken with Jammy Tomatoes, 32
BBQ sauce
    Slow Cooker BBQ Pulled Pork, 65
    Sweet & Sour Baked BBQ Chicken, 19
beef, 12
    Brisket for the Holidays, 54
    Crispy Garlic Butter Steak, 38
    Famous French Onion Meatloaf—Upgraded!, 38
    Giant Showstopping Meatballs in Rosé Sauce, 45
    Grilled Carne Asada with Homemade Salsa Roja, 46
    Jalapeño Popper–Stuffed Burgers with "Animal Sauce," 38
    Little Fancy Steak au Poivre, A, 53
    Low & Slow Texas Brisket Chili, 50
    Philly Cheesesteak—Hold the Bun!, 49
Belly-Warming Baked Broccoli Alfredo, 111
Best Damn Keto Pizza Ever!, The, 58
Blackened Salmon in Creamy Cajun Sauce, 83
bleu cheese, 20, 119. *See also* cheese
blueberries
    Triple Berry Crisp, 133
Bread Shop Broccoli Cheddar Soup, 92
Brisket for the Holidays, 54
broccoli
    Belly-Warming Baked Broccoli Alfredo, 111
    Bread Shop Broccoli Cheddar Soup, 92
    Homestyle Chicken-Bacon-Ranch Skillet, 31
Buffalo Chicken Pimento Dip, 152
burrata cheese, 32. *See also* cheese
butter, 11
    Belly-Warming Baked Broccoli Alfredo, 111
    Bread Shop Broccoli Cheddar Soup, 92
    Cauliflower Dirty Rice, 116
    Cheesy Garlic Breadsticks, 143
    Cinnamon Roll Cheesecake Bites, 125
    Classic Italian Chicken Marsala, 27

    Coconut Cake with Coconut Cream Cheese Frosting, 134
    Cozy Loaded "Potato" Soup, 88
    Creamy Smoked Cheddar "Grits," 115
    Crispy Garlic Butter Steak, 42
    Famous French Onion Meatloaf—Upgraded!, 38
    Filipino-Inspired Chicken Adobo, 28
    Garlic Lovers' Shrimp Scampi, 72
    Garlic Parmesan Green Beans, 112
    Giant Showstopping Meatballs in Rosé Sauce, 45
    Lemon Pound Cake with Lemony Cream Cheese Glaze, 126
    Little Fancy Steak au Poivre, A, 53
    Ooey Gooey Double Chocolate Brownies, 122
    Rich & Creamy Indian Butter Chicken, 24
    Sticky "Hot Honey" Chicken Wings, 20
    Stunning Brown Butter Shrimp & Grits, 76
    Triple Berry Crisp, 133
    Velvety Peanut Butter Cup Mousse with Homemade Chocolate Sauce, 129

C
Cajun seasoning
    Blackened Salmon in Creamy Cajun Sauce, 83
    Cauliflower Dirty Rice, 116
    Sausage, Peppers, & Onions with Spicy Creole Aioli, 66
canola, temperature for, 11
carrots
    5-Hour Short Rib Beef Stew, 95
    Buffalo Chicken Pimento Dip, 152
    "Hangover" Beef Pho, 99
    Mom's Chicken Soup, 96
    Sweet & Sour Baked BBQ Chicken, 19
Cauliflower Dirty Rice, 116
cheddar cheese, 41. *See also* cheese
cheese. *See also* American cheese; bleu cheese; burrata cheese; cheddar cheese; feta cheese; Italian-blend cheese; Oaxaca cheese; Swiss cheese
    Bacon & Bleu Coleslaw, 119
    Belly-Warming Baked Broccoli Alfredo, 111
    Blackened Salmon in Creamy Cajun Sauce, 83
    Bread Shop Broccoli Cheddar Soup, 92
    Buffalo Chicken Pimento Dip, 152
    Cheesy Garlic Breadsticks, 143
    Cheesy Low-Carb Scalloped "Potatoes," 104
    Cinnamon Roll Cheesecake Bites, 125
    Coconut Cake with Coconut Cream Cheese Frosting, 134
    Cozy Loaded "Potato" Soup, 88
    Everything-but-the-Bagel Dip, 156
    Famous French Onion Meatloaf—Upgraded!, 38
    Greek Roasted Garlic & Feta Dip, 160
    Guilt-Free Creamy Pasta Florentine, 69
    Homestyle Chicken- Bacon-Ranch Skillet, 31

Jalapeño Popper–Stuffed Burgers with "Animal Sauce," 41
Lemon Pound Cake with Lemony Cream Cheese Glaze, 126
Low-Carb Cheddar Bay Biscuits, 140
Million-Dollar Lasagna Roll-Ups, 62
Philly Cheesesteak—Hold the Bun!, 49
Quick & Easy Clam Chowder, 91
Restaurant-Style White Queso, 155
Sheet Pan Pesto Chicken with Jammy Tomatoes, 32
Spicy Maryland Crab Dip, 159
Sticky "Hot Honey" Chicken Wings, 20
Velvety Peanut Butter Cup Mousse with Homemade Chocolate Sauce, 129
Cheesy Garlic Breadsticks, 143
Cheesy Low-Carb Scalloped "Potatoes," 104
chicken
    bone-in, 19
    Buffalo Chicken Pimento Dip, 152
    Chinese Restaurant Sesame Chicken, 23
    Classic Italian Chicken Marsala, 27
    Filipino-Inspired Chicken Adobo, 28
    Homestyle Chicken-Bacon-Ranch Skillet, 24
    Pickle-Brined Crispy Chicken Tendies with Homemade Ranch, 16
    Rich & Creamy Indian Butter Chicken, 24
    Sheet Pan Pesto Chicken with Jammy Tomatoes, 32
    Slow Cooker BBQ Pulled Pork, 65
    Smoky Southwest Chicken Picante, 35
    Sticky "Hot Honey" Chicken Wings, 20
    Sweet & Sour Baked BBQ Chicken, 19
    temperature of, 12
    tenders, 16, 31
Chinese Restaurant Sesame Chicken, 23
chop styles, 9
cinnamon
    Cinnamon Roll Cheesecake Bites, 125
    Curried Butternut Squash Bisque, 100
    "Hangover" Beef Pho, 99
Cinnamon Roll Cheesecake Bites, 125
Classic Italian Chicken Marsala, 27
coconut aminos
    Chinese Restaurant Sesame Chicken, 23
    Grilled Carne Asada with Homemade Salsa Roja, 46
    Sticky "Hot Honey" Chicken Wings, 20
    Sweet Teriyaki-Glazed Salmon, 79
Coconut Cake with Coconut Cream Cheese Frosting, 134
coconut flour
    Chinese Restaurant Sesame Chicken, 23
    Cinnamon Roll Cheesecake Bites, 125
    Coconut Cake with Coconut Cream Cheese Frosting, 134
    Crispy Rosemary Sea Salt Crackers, 148
    Lemon Pound Cake with Lemony Cream Cheese Glaze, 126
coconut oil, 11
coffee
    Fall-Off-the-Bone Ribs with Mike's Coffee Dry Rub, 61

Cozy Loaded "Potato" Soup, 88
Crack Brussels Sprouts with Honey Mustard Sauce, 107
Creamy Smoked Cheddar "Grits," 115
Crispy Fried Fish Tacos with Baja Sauce, 75
Crispy Garlic Butter Steak, 38
Crispy Rosemary Sea Salt Crackers, 148, 156, 159, 160
Curried Butternut Squash Bisque, 100

D
deserts
    Cinnamon Roll Cheesecake Bites, 125
    Coconut Cake with Coconut Cream Cheese Frosting, 134
    Lemon Pound Cake with Lemony Cream Cheese Glaze, 126
    Magical Strawberry Icebox Pie, 137
    No-Churn Mint Chocolate Chip Ice Cream, 130
    Ooey Gooey Double Chocolate Brownies, 122
    Triple Berry Crisp, 133
    Velvety Peanut Butter Cup Mousse with Homemade Chocolate Sauce, 129
dips
    Buffalo Chicken Pimento Dip, 152
    Everything-but-the-Bagel Dip, 156
    Greek Roasted Garlic & Feta Dip, 159
    Restaurant-Style White Queso, 155
    Spicy Maryland Crab Dip, 159

E
eggs
    Best Damn Keto Pizza Ever!, The, 58
    Cheesy Garlic Breadsticks, 143
    Chinese Restaurant Sesame Chicken, 23
    Crispy Rosemary Sea Salt Crackers, 148
    Famous French Onion Meatloaf— Upgraded!, 38
    Fluffy Waffles & Pancakes, 147
    Giant Showstopping Meatballs in Rosé Sauce, 45
    Keto Cornbread, 144
    Lemon Pound Cake with Lemony Cream Cheese Glaze, 126
    Low-Carb Cheddar Bay Biscuits, 140
    Magical Strawberry Icebox Pie, 137
    No-Churn Mint Chocolate Chip Ice Cream, 130
    Ooey Gooey Double Chocolate Brownies, 122
    Sugarless Shrimp Pad Thai, 80
erythritol, 10
Everything-but-the-Bagel Dip, 156

F
Fall-Off-the-Bone Ribs with Mike's Coffee Dry Rub, 61
Famous French Onion Meatloaf— Upgraded!, 38
fat, 11
feta cheese, 160. See also cheese
Filipino-Inspired Chicken Adobo, 28
fish. See also seafood

Blackened Salmon in Creamy Cajun Sauce, 83
Crispy Fried Fish Tacos with Baja Sauce, 75
Everything-but-the-Bagel Dip, 156
Pepper-Crusted Tuna Steak with Sesame Ginger Chimichurri, 84
sauce, 80, 99
Sweet Teriyaki-Glazed Salmon, 79
temperature for, 12
flaky (finishing) salt, 10
Fluffy Waffles & Pancakes, 147

G
game meats, 12
garam masala
    Rich & Creamy Indian Butter Chicken, 24
Garlic Lovers' Shrimp Scampi, 72
Garlic Parmesan Green Beans, 112
ghee, 11
Giant Showstopping Meatballs in Rosé Sauce, 45
ginger powder
    Curried Butternut Squash Bisque, 100
granulated sweetener
    5-Hour Short Rib Beef Stew, 95
    Bacon & Bleu Coleslaw, 119
    Coconut Cake with Coconut Cream Cheese Frosting, 134
    Crack Brussels Sprouts with Honey Mustard Sauce, 107
    Creamy Smoked Cheddar "Grits," 115
    Fluffy Waffles & Pancakes, 147
    Giant Showstopping Meatballs in Rosé Sauce, 45
    "Hangover" Beef Pho, 99
    Jalapeño Popper–Stuffed Burgers with "Animal Sauce," 38
    Keto Cornbread, 144
    Lemon Pound Cake with Lemony Cream Cheese Glaze, 126
    Low-Carb Cheddar Bay Biscuits, 140
    Magical Strawberry Icebox Pie, 137
    Rich & Creamy Indian Butter Chicken, 24
    Triple Berry Crisp, 133
    Velvety Peanut Butter Cup Mousse with Homemade Chocolate Sauce, 129
grapeseed oils, 11
Greek Roasted Garlic & Feta Dip, 159
Greek yogurt
    Curried Butternut Squash Bisque, 100
    Greek Roasted Garlic & Feta Dip, 160
    Rich & Creamy Indian Butter Chicken, 24
Grilled Carne Asada with Homemade Salsa Roja, 46
Gruyère
    Famous French Onion Meatloaf— Upgraded!, 38
Guilt-Free Creamy Pasta Florentine, 69

H
"Hangover" Beef Pho, 99
Homestyle Chicken-Bacon-Ranch Skillet, 24
"Hot Honey" sauce, 20

I

Italian-blend cheese, 31. See also cheese
Italian herb
    Belly-Warming Baked Broccoli Alfredo, 111
    Cheesy Garlic Breadsticks, 143
    Famous French Onion Meatloaf—Upgraded!, 38
    Guilt-Free Creamy Pasta Florentine, 69
    Million-Dollar Lasagna Roll-Ups, 62

J

Jalapeño Popper–Stuffed Burgers with "Animal Sauce," 38
jalapeño
    Grilled Carne Asada with Homemade Salsa Roja, 46
    "Hangover" Beef Pho, 99
    Jalapeño Popper–Stuffed Burgers with "Animal Sauce," 41
    Low & Slow Texas Brisket Chili, 50
    Restaurant-Style White Queso, 155
julienne, 9

K

Keto Cornbread, 144
knife cuts, 9
kohlrabi
    Cheesy Low-Carb Scalloped "Potatoes," 104
kosher salt, 10
    Brisket for the Holidays, 54
    Crispy Garlic Butter Steak, 42
    Little Fancy Steak au Poivre, A, 53
    Smoky Southwest Chicken Picante, 35

L

Lemon Pound Cake with Lemony Cream Cheese Glaze, 126
Little Fancy Steak au Poivre, A, 53
Low-Carb Cheddar Bay Biscuits, 140
Low & Slow Texas Brisket Chili, 50

M

Magical Strawberry Icebox Pie, 137
mayonnaise
    Bacon & Bleu Coleslaw, 119
    Buffalo Chicken Pimento Dip, 152
    Crack Brussels Sprouts with Honey Mustard Sauce, 107
    Crispy Fried Fish Tacos with Baja Sauce, 75
    Jalapeño Popper–Stuffed Burgers with "Animal Sauce," 38
    Philly Cheesesteak—Hold the Bun!, 49
    Pickle-Brined Crispy Chicken Tendies with Homemade Ranch, 16
    "Potato" Salad, 108
    Sausage, Peppers, & Onions with Spicy Creole Aioli, 66
    Spicy Maryland Crab Dip, 159
Million-Dollar Lasagna Roll-Ups, 62
mince style, 9
mise en place, 8

monk fruit, 10
mozzarella
    Belly-Warming Baked Broccoli Alfredo, 111
    Best Damn Keto Pizza Ever!, The, 58
    Cheesy Garlic Breadsticks, 143
    Homestyle Chicken-Bacon-Ranch Skillet, 31
    Million-Dollar Lasagna Roll-Ups, 62
    Restaurant-Style White Queso, 155
    Sheet Pan Pesto Chicken with Jammy Tomatoes, 32
mushrooms
    Blackened Salmon in Creamy Cajun Sauce, 83
    Classic Italian Chicken Marsala, 27
    Guilt-Free Creamy Pasta Florentine, 69
    Philly Cheesesteak—Hold the Bun!, 49
mustard. See yellow mustard

N

No-Churn Mint Chocolate Chip Ice Cream, 130
noodles
    Guilt-Free Creamy Pasta Florentine, 69
    "Hangover" Beef Pho, 99
    Palmini, 69
    shirataki, 80, 99
    Sugarless Shrimp Pad Thai, 80
    zucchini, 69

O

Oaxaca cheese, 155. See also cheese
Old Bay Seasoning
    Quick & Easy Clam Chowder, 91
    Spicy Maryland Crab Dip, 159
    Stunning Brown Butter Shrimp & Grits, 76
olive oil
    Curried Butternut Squash Bisque, 100
    Garlic Lovers' Shrimp Scampi, 72
    Greek Roasted Garlic & Feta Dip, 160
    Sheet Pan Pesto Chicken with Jammy Tomatoes, 32
    temperature for, 11
onion. See also yellow onions
    Rich & Creamy Indian Butter Chicken, 24
    Smoky Southwest Chicken Picante, 35
    Sweet & Sour Baked BBQ Chicken, 19
Ooey Gooey Double Chocolate Brownies, 122
oregano
    Best Damn Keto Pizza Ever!, The, 58
    Giant Showstopping Meatballs in Rosé Sauce, 45
    Greek Roasted Garlic & Feta Dip, 160
    Grilled Carne Asada with Homemade Salsa Roja, 46
    Homestyle Chicken-Bacon-Ranch Skillet, 31
    Sausage, Peppers, & Onions with Spicy Creole Aioli, 66

P

paprika
    Blackened Salmon in Creamy Cajun Sauce, 83
    Brisket for the Holidays, 54
    Cauliflower Dirty Rice, 116
    Curried Butternut Squash Bisque, 100
    Fall-Off-the-Bone Ribs with Mike's Coffee Dry Rub, 61
    Famous French Onion Meatloaf—Upgraded!, 38
    Grilled Carne Asada with Homemade Salsa Roja, 46
    Low & Slow Texas Brisket Chili, 50
    Sausage, Peppers, & Onions with Spicy Creole Aioli, 66
    Slow Cooker BBQ Pulled Pork, 65
    Sticky "Hot Honey" Chicken Wings, 20
    Stunning Brown Butter Shrimp & Grits, 76
Parmesan. See also cheese
    Belly-Warming Baked Broccoli Alfredo, 111
    Best Damn Keto Pizza Ever!, The, 58
    Cheesy Garlic Breadsticks, 143
    Cheesy Low-Carb Scalloped "Potatoes," 104
    Classic Italian Chicken Marsala, 27
    Crispy Fried Fish Tacos with Baja Sauce, 75
    Crispy Rosemary Sea Salt Crackers, 148
    Garlic Parmesan Green Beans, 112
    Giant Showstopping Meatballs in Rosé Sauce, 45
    Guilt-Free Creamy Pasta Florentine, 69
    Low-Carb Cheddar Bay Biscuits, 140
    Million-Dollar Lasagna Roll-Ups, 62
    Pickle-Brined Crispy Chicken Tendies with Homemade Ranch, 16
peanut
    Sugarless Shrimp Pad Thai, 80
    temperature for, 11
    Velvety Peanut Butter Cup Mousse with Homemade Chocolate Sauce, 129
peppercorns
    Filipino-Inspired Chicken Adobo, 28
    Little Fancy Steak au Poivre, A, 53
    Pepper-Crusted Tuna Steak with Sesame Ginger Chimichurri, 84
    Slow Cooker BBQ Pulled Pork, 65
Pepper-Crusted Tuna Steak with Sesame Ginger Chimichurri, 84
Philly Cheesesteak—Hold the Bun!, 49
Pickle-Brined Crispy Chicken Tendies with Homemade Ranch, 16
pizza
    The Best Damn Keto Pizza Ever!, 58
pork, 12
    Crispy Fried Fish Tacos with Baja Sauce, 75
    Pickle-Brined Crispy Chicken Tendies with Homemade Ranch, 16
    Restaurant-Style White Queso, 155
    Slow Cooker BBQ Pulled Pork, 65
    Spicy Maryland Crab Dip, 159
"Potato" Salad, 108
provolone cheese. See also cheese
    Philly Cheesesteak—Hold the Bun!, 49

Q

Quick & Easy Clam Chowder, 88

R

raspberries
　Triple Berry Crisp, 133
Restaurant-Style White Queso, 155
ribs
　5-Hour Short Rib Beef Stew, 95
　Cauliflower Dirty Rice, 116
　Fall-Off-the-Bone Ribs with Mike's
　　Coffee Dry Rub, 61
　Mom's Chicken Soup, 96
Rich & Creamy Indian Butter Chicken, 24
rosemary
　5-Hour Short Rib Beef Stew, 95
　Crispy Garlic Butter Steak, 42
　Crispy Rosemary Sea Salt Crackers,
　　148
　Everything-but-the-Bagel Dip, 156
　Greek Roasted Garlic & Feta Dip, 160
　Spicy Maryland Crab Dip, 159
rutabaga
　Cheesy Low-Carb Scalloped
　　"Potatoes," 104

S

salmon. See also seafood
　Blackened Salmon in Creamy Cajun
　　Sauce, 83
　Everything-but-the-Bagel Dip, 156
　Sweet Teriyaki-Glazed Salmon, 79
　temperature for, 12
salts, 10
salted butter. See butter
San Marzano tomatoes, 45. See also
　tomato
Sausage, Peppers, & Onions with Spicy
　Creole Aioli, 66
seafood
　Blackened Salmon in Creamy Cajun
　　Sauce, 83
　Crispy Fried Fish Tacos with Baja
　　Sauce, 75
　Garlic Lovers' Shrimp Scampi, 72
　Pepper-Crusted Tuna Steak with Sesame
　　Ginger Chimichurri, 84
　Stunning Brown Butter Shrimp & Grits,
　　76
　Sugarless Shrimp Pad Thai, 80
　Sweet Teriyaki-Glazed Salmon, 79
sesame oil
　Chinese Restaurant Sesame Chicken,
　　23
　Pepper-Crusted Tuna Steak with Sesame
　　Ginger Chimichurri, 84
　temperature for, 11
sesame seeds
　Chinese Restaurant Sesame Chicken,
　　23
　Pepper-Crusted Tuna Steak with Sesame
　　Ginger Chimichurri, 84
　Sweet Teriyaki-Glazed Salmon, 79
Sheet Pan Pesto Chicken with Jammy
　Tomatoes, 32
shrimps. See also seafood

Garlic Lovers' Shrimp Scampi, 72
Stunning Brown Butter Shrimp & Grits,
　76
Sugarless Shrimp Pad Thai, 80
slices types, 9
Slow Cooker BBQ Pulled Pork, 65
Smoky Southwest Chicken Picante, 35
soups
　5-Hour Short Rib Beef Stew, 95
　Bread Shop Broccoli Cheddar Soup,
　　92
　Cozy Loaded "Potato" Soup, 88
　Curried Butternut Squash Bisque, 100
　"Hangover" Beef Pho, 99
　Quick & Easy Clam Chowder, 88
soy sauce
　Chinese Restaurant Sesame Chicken,
　　23
　Filipino-Inspired Chicken Adobo, 28
　Grilled Carne Asada with Homemade
　　Salsa Roja, 46
　Sticky "Hot Honey" Chicken Wings, 20
　Sweet Teriyaki-Glazed Salmon, 79
Spicy Maryland Crab Dip, 159
stevia, 10
Sticky "Hot Honey" Chicken Wings, 20
Stunning Brown Butter Shrimp & Grits, 76
Sugarless Shrimp Pad Thai, 80
sweetener, 10. See also allulose sweetener;
　erythritol; monk fruit; stevia
Sweet & Sour Baked BBQ Chicken, 19
Sweet Teriyaki-Glazed Salmon, 79
Swiss cheese, 38, 49. See also cheese

T

table salt (iodized), 10
Tajín chili-lime seasoning
　Crispy Fried Fish Tacos with Baja
　　Sauce, 75
temperatures for meat preparation, 12
tomato
　5-Hour Short Rib Beef Stew, 95
　Cauliflower Dirty Rice, 116
　Giant Showstopping Meatballs in Rosé
　　Sauce, 45
　Grilled Carne Asada with Homemade
　　Salsa Roja, 46
　Jalapeño Popper–Stuffed Burgers with
　　"Animal Sauce," 41
　Low & Slow Texas Brisket Chili, 50
　Sausage, Peppers, & Onions with Spicy
　　Creole Aioli, 66
　Sheet Pan Pesto Chicken with Jammy
　　Tomatoes, 32
　Smoky Southwest Chicken Picante, 35
tomato sauce
　Rich & Creamy Indian Butter Chicken,
　　24
　Slow Cooker BBQ Pulled Pork, 65
Triple Berry Crisp, 133
tuna. See also seafood
　Pepper-Crusted Tuna Steak with Sesame
　　Ginger Chimichurri, 84

U

unsalted butter. See butter

V

veggie dishes, 11
　Bacon & Bleu Coleslaw, 119
　Belly-Warming Baked Broccoli Alfredo,
　　111
　Cauliflower Dirty Rice, 116
　Cheesy Low-Carb Scalloped
　　"Potatoes," 104
　Crack Brussels Sprouts with Honey
　　Mustard Sauce, 107
　Creamy Smoked Cheddar "Grits," 115
　Garlic Parmesan Green Beans, 112
　"Potato" Salad, 108
Velvety Peanut Butter Cup Mousse with
　Homemade Chocolate Sauce, 129

W

wings
　Sticky "Hot Honey" Chicken Wings, 20
Worcestershire sauce
　Brisket for the Holidays, 54
　Philly Cheesesteak—Hold the Bun!, 49
　Slow Cooker BBQ Pulled Pork, 65

X

xanthan gum
　Best Damn Keto Pizza Ever!, The, 58
　Bread Shop Broccoli Cheddar Soup,
　　92
　Classic Italian Chicken Marsala, 27
　Fluffy Waffles & Pancakes, 147
　No-Churn Mint Chocolate Chip Ice
　　Cream, 130

Y

yellow mustard
　Fall-Off-the-Bone Ribs with Mike's
　　Coffee Dry Rub, 61
　Famous French Onion Meatloaf—
　　Upgraded!, 38
　Sticky "Hot Honey" Chicken Wings, 20
yellow onions
　5-Hour Short Rib Beef Stew, 95
　Bread Shop Broccoli Cheddar Soup,
　　92
　Brisket for the Holidays, 54
　Cauliflower Dirty Rice, 116
　Cheesy Low-Carb Scalloped
　　"Potatoes," 104
　Cozy Loaded "Potato" Soup, 88
　Greek Roasted Garlic & Feta Dip, 159
　"Hangover" Beef Pho, 99
　Low & Slow Texas Brisket Chili, 50
　Philly Cheesesteak—Hold the Bun!, 49
　Quick & Easy Clam Chowder, 88
　Sausage, Peppers, & Onions with Spicy
　　Creole Aioli, 66
yogurt. See Greek yogurt